COUNTRY DOCTOR

Essays in Memory of
Walter E. Eells, M.D.

by Robert J. Eells

ISBN: 0-75961-854-2

This book is printed on acid free paper.

1stBooks - rev. 4/10/01

Walter E. Eells, 1971

DEDICATION:

For Eleanor (Eells) Gray, loving and faithful daughter of Walter E. Eells. Sister: any father would be blessed to have a daughter like you.

TABLE OF CONTENTS

ACKNOWLEDGMENTS

During my father's final twenty-five months, he received wonderful round-the-clock home care from many women. This gave me more time to discover new stories for the third edition. Special thanks, then, go to Cheryle Askerzadah, Shirley Bowker, Nancy Latourette, Carol Reade, Daisey Wagner, and Joan Williams. My cousin, Beverly McCready, kept the office running smoothly and surrounded her uncle and aunt with emotional support. Rev. Joseph Hill and my cousin, Carolyn Dellwo, made valuable written contributions. My secretary, Betty Videto, was very supportive and worked miracles with the word processor. Finally, Spring Arbor College gave me some extra free time as part of my recent sabbatical. Thanks, again, to all.

BIOGRAPHICAL SKETCH

Walter E. Eells, M.D., 1902-2000

My book could also easily be entitled, "Twentieth Century Doctor," for this country physician's life spanned almost the entire century. Walter was born on August 28, 1902, joining an older brother, Benjamin, and became the middle child a couple of years later with the arrival of a sister, Evelyn. His father, Clarence, and mother, Carrie (Bump) Eells, were Waltonians, and Walter made Walton, New York the center of his life and practice. Clarence—who died when Walter was five—worked in retail, and Carrie kept busy as a midwife. Carrie's work would eventually lead to the establishment of Smith Hospital, named for Walter's stepfather, Dr. William Smith.

Carrie's midwifery no doubt played a role in convincing young Walter to pursue a medical career. By his high school years, he had already made such a commitment. Nothing else ever appealed very much to him in terms of a future vocation. Walter was a hard-working student at Walton Central High School, graduating in 1920. However, he felt that he needed to lift his grades a bit, so he spent an extra year at WHS in order to win a scholarship to college. He was successful and entered Cornell University in 1921. After completing undergraduate work, he entered Albany Medical School in 1925, receiving an M.D. in 1929. Upon completion of an internship at Binghamton General Hospital, he began his medical practice in Walton on June 1, 1930.

Walter's practice lasted more than sixty years. Fairly soon after arriving in Walton, he purchased his home at 35 Townsend Street—a home which already contained a medical suite on the first floor. Shortly thereafter he was also working at his own Smith Hospital directly across the street from his home. This kind of combination made him unique, not only in Walton but probably just about everywhere. From this context—over such an extensive period—Walter cared for tens of thousands of patients, performed hundreds of operations, and helped bring over 2,000 babies into the world!

Walter was proud of his many medical "firsts," including being the first Walton physician to operate and to use penicillin. He knew his limitations, though, and never attempted major surgery of any kind. When major problems arose, he loved to consult with specialists and surgeons from Oneonta, Cooperstown, and Binghamton, and frequently assisted them as they performed surgeries at Smith or Delaware Valley Hospitals.

During his long career, Walter was known for his community and church involvement. For example, he served for over twenty years on the boards of Walton Central School, the vocational school (BOCES), and Ogden Free Library. He was also a trustee and loyal member of the Walton Reformed Presbyterian Church.

Throughout his life, Walter gave generously to individuals, charities, and church programs of all kinds. Helping financially became one of his favorite activities.

During the latter part of his career, Walter received many awards for his medical practice and community service—from local, county, and state organizations. Accolades seemed to come in bunches every ten years, beginning in 1960. He was very proud of the fact that Walton honored him as its 1980 "Man of the Year."

Though he took little time off during his early career, as the years unfolded he did find outlets in board games (especially Scrabble), in reading historical novels, in traveling, and in the final passion of his life—editing the bulletin of the Eells Family Association.

Katherine Henderson became his wife on September 9, 1939. She quickly transformed herself into a "girl Friday" in every respect. They were truly a medical team, though Katherine had no formal medical training. Their marriage produced three children: Eleanor, Robert, and Kenneth. The children eventually gave them eight grandchildren, and at the time of his death one great-grandchild was on the way.

Walter's long and productive life came to an end on January 20, 2000. He and Katherine had been living at home receiving round-the-clock care from several women after he suffered a heart attack in late December 1997. He rallied many times following his heart attack and amazed us all with his determination and his constant love for family and friends. He continued, of course, to win most of the Scrabble games until the very end. How do you spell "grace"?

PART I

Essays and Comments
from

COUNTRY DOCTOR

First Edition
(1992)

Robert J. Eells

A TWINKLE IN HIS EYE

It was past midnight and the late movie wasn't very good, so I decided to head for bed. "Dad," I whispered, "isn't it time to call it a night?" He kept typing. I repeated the question. "Soon, Bob," he finally answered, "I only have one or two insurance forms to complete. Besides, I have a delivery across the street, and don't you know what time of the night babies like to be born? About the time my head hits the pillow the phone will ring."

I didn't say anything, hoping he would forget about me. I was tired; besides, I had already helped with a couple of births since this was one of my summer breaks when I was still contemplating a medical career.

My own head hadn't been on the pillow for very long when the first hint of trouble occurred: the loud, annoying sound of a ringing phone. It was so jarring, even in my room, that I was immediately awake. Why Dad slept a foot away from this monster was a mystery to me.

Another familiar sound reached me—shuffling feet on the hallway carpet as Dad made his way to the bathroom. He didn't close the door. The splashing of urine in the toilet also reminded me that I was home from college (my bathroom there was many rooms distant from my bedroom). Then I really got tense. Will he remember me or shuffle on back to dress and hurry across the street to the hospital and confront the "why-do-you-have-to-be-born-now" baby?

My semi-consciousness took command. The sheet came up, the head ducked beneath the pillow; had I been fully awake the fingers would have been crossed. Silence. It seemed like minutes before...the muffled knock.

"Bob, are you awake?" Silence. "Bob, would you like to help with this delivery?" I exhaled. "Sure, Dad. I'll be dressed in a minute."

Feeling sorry for myself, I dressed, slapped some cold water on my face and headed across to the delivery room—on the first floor of Smith Hospital. Dad, of course, was already there.

I washed and put on my gown and entered the room. The woman was already on the table. One nurse was present. Dad had given the spinal block and the mother-to-be was doing her best to push, despite the numbing effect of the drug. I didn't know then exactly what was expected of me so I kept back a little bit out of the way, just waiting and observing.

Before too long I realized that something was wrong. It wasn't going according to "schedule"; this was going to be a difficult birth. Dad kept working—examining, probing, checking, encouraging. But little seemed to be happening.

My first job came with a familiar request. "Bob," my father grimaced, "would you rub my back? It's bothering me from all the bending." So I came around behind him and massaged his aching back.

Dad looked concerned. His frown turned into a different request: "Bob, get behind, I mean beside, her and push."

"Push?" I questioned.

"Yes, push," he repeated matter-of-factly.

So I placed myself beside this struggling patient and started to push.

"More firmly," ordered the doctor. "We've got to help her force the baby out. And reach under the sheet. Place your hands directly on her belly." I hesitated, but only briefly; this was no time for embarrassment by anyone.

So the woman strained, and I pushed, and Dad pulled, and, finally, the baby arrived.

Relieved and even more tired, I stepped back, fully expecting to retire gracefully. But again something was wrong. It took me a moment or two to identify what it was: the baby had made no sound. No crying, no gasping for breath.

Then I took my first real look at the baby and my heart sank. It was blue and lifeless. No sound, no motion, wrong color. Dear God, I prayed silently, don't let this baby die.

4

My father swung into action. First he placed the baby on a separate table. Then he checked the air passage, inserting a device through which he breathed into the limp form. He rubbed the baby's hands and feet, inverted the infant to slap its bottom, and began a process of regular breathing into the baby's mouth.

Still no response. He checked for any signs of a heartbeat, thought he detected a slight sound, and returned to his methodical efforts. The minutes dragged on. I glanced at the nurse who was attending to the woman and caught her look of worry, even hopelessness.

Still no response. "Bob," said Dad, "we've got to try something different. Go into the prep room and get two pans. Fill one with cold water and one with warm water and bring them here. Hurry." I carried out the order, trying to discern what was being planned.

After receiving the water-filled pans, Dad began a new procedure: first he placed the baby neck-high into the cold water, then into the warm water, then rubbed hands and feet, and finally breathed into the baby's mouth. He repeated this ritual several more times, then checked for the faint heartbeat. Again and again the ritual took place, until it all became a blur. Time seemed to stand still.

At one point I almost blurted out my frustration, but I bit my tongue. Surely he knows what he's doing, I wondered in desperation.

I had turned aside and was rubbing my own back when I thought I heard a sound. Nothing? There it was again, audible and distinct—the sound of air being drawn into lungs. Then the sound of crying, a baby's cry, first weak, then quickly strengthening. The most wonderful sound I had ever heard, given these circumstances.

I could hardly believe my ears. For a moment I was immobilized. I didn't dare move for fear of breaking the "spell" and discovering it had been only a dream. But I returned to the table with the two quick steps—lively steps now—and confirmed the reality of the miracle I had just witnessed: a no-longer-blue baby crying with gusto and a mother with the biggest smile on her face and with tears streaming down her cheeks. She wasn't the only one with wet cheeks.

I wanted to shout and give Dad a big hug, but I did neither. Maybe it was my shyness or Dad's bad back; maybe just the Eells "reserve." I do remember saying something about the happy outcome. And I'll never forget his response: "Bob," he said with a twinkle in his eye, "she already has three sons, and she really wanted this girl." She really wanted this girl. What a typical answer from such an atypical man!

Well, here's the hug, Dad, in essay form from me, from the mother and her daughter, from your tireless and supportive wife, from your other two children and grandchildren, from your patients, and from all the Eellses everywhere.

FLIGHT FOR LIFE

He already felt like a big shot: at twelve, oldest of five children, their leader and benefactor. It was he who showed them how to play catch, to work the TV, and how to swipe cookies while looking innocent. He enjoyed playing the role of big brother. He bragged about how he was always the first to try anything new or dangerous—especially dangerous. He was a big shot with courage.

So, when his mother reminded all the children in late August that it was time to get their school physicals, he didn't think much about it at first. When his younger brother started to cause a fuss about visiting the doctor, he comforted him. "It's no big deal," crowed the big brother. "Nothing to be afraid about. I've been there before. We all have."

"But what about shots?" whined the sibling. "I hate shots!"

"They don't hurt that much," came the confident sounding reply as the eldest placed his arm around the shoulders of the doubter. It wasn't quite that simple, he knew, as he recalled how getting shots was not his favorite activity either. But now was no time to show any weakness.

The fateful day came and they all headed off to see Doc Eells. Everything went smoothly for awhile. Kids were weighed, poked, probed, examined up and down. Hearts and lungs sounded fine. Eyes, ears, noses, and throats all passed the test. And the big shot was always first to be examined at every point.

The other children, though, began to get a little nervous. Finally, one whispered to the eldest, "Do you think he forgot about the shots? I hope so." Even their leader began to hope.

But their hopes were dashed when the doctor declared, "Everything is fine. All that remain are their shots. We'll be finished in just a couple of minutes." The children paled; even big brother gulped as his eyes followed the doctor departing the room to prepare the first injection. From that "dungeon" came the inquiry, "Who wants to be first?"

"Me, Doc," came the response from the eldest, though his heart began to race and his knees felt a little weak. "Shots don't bother me," he said to the others in the room, hoping that no one heard the squeak in his voice or sensed his own anxiety.

All pretense collapsed though as the doctor re-entered the room with the needle. Not any needle, but the largest needle the big shot had ever seen! Panic set in as the doctor approached. Not this time, not with THAT needle, he thought, picturing it going all the way through his arm. He had to act and act fast.

Just as the doctor reached for his arm, he bolted. Out of the examining room, past several startled patients in the waiting room, bursting through the screen door. Down the steps he ran, out to the sidewalk. Then he hesitated. Which way to turn? Right, turn right and head downtown, came the mind's snap judgment. He quickly discovered, however, that turning left might have been wiser.

Turning right placed him in the direct path of the mailman a few yards away. Only then, as he picked up speed, did he glance over his shoulder to witness the terrifying sight: Doc Eells too had rushed out of the office, <u>needle in hand</u>, following him down the sidewalk!

"Stop that boy," yelled the doctor. Not once but twice. Now the big shot was only a step or two away from the bemused mailman who had been watching the whole brief episode. Another step—around the mailman—and he would be free. Then something horrible happened. Just as he swerved to avoid the obstacle, an arm came down around his wrist, pulling him up off his feet.

"I've got him, Doc," the mailman called out. "He won't be going anywhere."

"Hold him there, and watch out for his legs," panted Doc Eells as he arrived on the scene.

Then came the greatest indignity of all: the big shot got shot, right on the sidewalk, arms pinned down, helpless, right in front of several people viewing the event from across the street in front of Smith Hospital. The shot hurt, but the disgrace was even worse, especially as he turned to see that his brothers and sisters had also seen everything from the office porch.

"Now, that didn't hurt all that much, did it," stated the doctor as he withdrew the monstrous needle and walked back to the office as if this sort of thing happened every day.

COMMON SENSE

As a country doctor, Dad knew very well how unpredictable the timing of new babies can be. Many years of experience had taught him that some babies arrive early; they can't wait to investigate the world around them. Some babies are punctual; they are very proper and well-behaved from the start. Others, well, others have a tough time saying good-bye to such a secure environment. They'd rather be late, thank you.

So it was not unusual for Dad to wait for this particular woman to deliver her baby in the mid-1950s. Smith Hospital's maternity ward was a comfortable place to reside, anticipating the happy day. As the days dragged on, though, it became a matter of some concern. Being one or two days late beyond the due date is no problem, if all the signs are positive. Even one week is usually not a reason for panic. At ten days, however, when the woman was admitted, Dad no doubt began to frown. When the two-week period had been reached, something had to be initiated.

Drugs were an option, drugs to stimulate labor. But Dad usually hesitated to use them, preferring to let nature take its course. He had performed a number of Caesareans by then, but this boundary too he crossed reluctantly. A Caesarean was pretty major surgery and complications were possible. Nonetheless, something had to be done to get things moving along.

A country doctor, happily, has several other options available to him, especially when he owns a hospital right across the street from his home. One night as Dad made his rounds, and after checking the woman's static condition, a plan emerged in his fertile mind.

"Hello," whispered the doctor as he entered the maternity ward about midnight. "Thought I'd stop by again to see how you're doing." The woman was, understandably, having difficulty sleeping.

Dad checked her vital signs again, then stopped back to "check out" her room. "You know," he continued somewhat sadly, "this room doesn't look too sharp. Look at the paint. It's peeling in several places. And look here where the beds have been repeatedly slammed against the wall. Those spots could really use some help. I have an idea. I'll be right back."

The doctor returned about fifteen minutes later with a bucket of paint, a brush, and some rags. He arranged his equipment and started to paint the wall.

"Say," he inquired a few minutes later, "why don't you help me? I'm dropping some paint on the floor. Would you wipe up those drops for me?" The woman hardly hesitated a second, struggling off the bed and sliding down to her knees. After all, this was a hospital and he was a doctor!

This unique couple continued painting and wiping until they had finished one wall of the room. By then the woman had been on her feet, up and down, many times. Dad then removed the material from the room and thanked his assistant for her help. I'm sure he knew what was going to happen shortly.

The baby arrived a few hours later. Dad didn't get much sleep that night, but he didn't really mind.

OOPS!

Dad and his office assistant trained me in the laboratory to perform simple tests on blood and urine. We were looking for such things as sugar in the urine or evidence of abnormalities in the blood that could be seen with a low-power microscope. Nothing fancy but very effective, as far as general practice is concerned. After awhile I became pretty good at administering these tests. My confidence also soared when Dad showed me how to remove blood from a patient's arm, with tourniquet and needle. Upon mastering this procedure, I was really beginning to feel like a medical student. How quickly, though, the proud stumble and fall.

One day Dad called me into his office and asked me to do him a favor by driving up the street a block or two and obtaining a blood sample from someone. I quickly agreed since this procedure was now in my repertoire. "Who's the patient?" I asked. When he supplied the name, I was both thrilled and nervous. It was a young woman on whom I'd had a crush for several years. She was then a senior in high school and gorgeous, at least to me. I was nervous just thinking about being in her presence. But now was the time to impress her with my knowledge and skills, my collegiate sophistication.

It was a beautiful day; late spring was breaking out everywhere. With a pounding heart I knocked on her door. There she was—smiling and stuff. She didn't look sick to me. I wanted someone to poke me with a pin to see if this was all a dream. She ushered me into the house, and I quickly sat down so that she wouldn't see my knees were shaking.

We exchanged pleasantries. My mouth got dry. Making small talk with a princess wasn't easy. I almost forgot my reason for visiting. "Oh," I finally blurted out, "I'd better get some blood." She offered me her arm, the loveliest arm I had ever seen. I hesitated to touch it because my fingers were ice cold.

Somehow I managed to tie off the tourniquet. I reached for the needle and gently, carefully inserted it into the biggest vein in her arm. I asked her if it hurt. "Not much," she replied, with that disarming, distracting smile. Without thinking, lost in her gaze, I continued the familiar procedure.

Then I froze. Something was wrong, dead wrong, I feared. What an idiot! I screamed to myself, contemplating what had just occurred. I had inserted a needle which still had air remaining in it, then squeezed out the excess into her vein! Air in a vein could lead to death, I remembered. Isn't this the way ingenious criminals silence their hapless victims?

"Bob, are you waiting for me to hurt before you finish?" she laughed. I gulped and finished drawing the blood. I've killed her! I thought. She's going to die and it's my fault. How could I have been so stupid? I said my good-byes. But now her smile seemed to be mocking me. How long will it take, I wondered as I drove back to the office. Will she die in a few minutes, or maybe in an hour or two? Tomorrow?

I couldn't keep it a secret. Dad had to be confronted with my blunder. Maybe he could do something. Maybe there was an antidote. Briefly I relived my horror story with him. He listened quietly.

"Will she die?" I asked, desperate for absolution. Then came the most soothing words I had ever heard. "Bob, don't worry. That amount of air in her system won't do any damage."

I wanted to kiss him, but I was so drained of energy that I couldn't move. No death, no manslaughter charges, no prison. What a relief it was!

I must admit, though, that in the following days, whenever the phone rang I got mighty anxious. Moral of this story: Never send a young man in "puppy love" to do a man's work. The young woman, by the way, is still very much alive.

AFFIRMATION

The afternoon was long and hot. Sweat poured down my face, mingling with the dust and debris from the bales of hay I was throwing and placing into position. The cool spring water from my grandfather's milk house had never tasted better. But I was tired and needed more than liquid refreshment; I needed, like any good college student, a nap. I closed my eyes and pictured myself lying comfortably on my bed as a gentle breeze from a fan wafted over my body. A smile crossed my face.

But the nap was not to be, at least not as soon as desired. When I arrived home, I parked the car in the back and tried to sneak through the kitchen and up the back stairs to my room. Sneaking was necessary because my father's office was full—as usual—and if I wasn't careful he would see me and direct me into his office to "observe" something and the nap would be but a fond memory.

Past the laboratory door up the stairs, into the tub for a brief shower; I thought that I had made it. I was safe. Just as I entered my room, though, came the voice: "Bob, are you up there?" called my father. "Can you come down for a minute? I need some help in the office." I groaned, dressed, and headed down the stairs.

I avoided going through the full waiting room and entered by way of the laboratory. Dad was already busy in the examining room. A woman had brought in her daughter, who had been in an accident. She had suffered a cut on her face, which appeared to be about two inches in length. It was jagged and fairly deep. A nasty-looking wound.

Dad had me wash up and help him by handing him instruments and cutting suture in the right place (I always hoped it was "right"). He worked in silence for a few minutes. The mother, however, was very distressed, pacing back and forth, muttering about the cut and the inevitable scar it would produce, and how tragic this was for her pretty young daughter who was

14

just entering her teens. Naturally, this upset the girl who soon was crying softly, with tears dribbling down both cheeks.

Abruptly, Dad turned and asked the mother to leave the room. She stopped pacing, glanced at the doctor...and left. Dad then began talking to me or, rather, to the young woman through me. He told me how some doctors hurry a procedure like this one, taking shortcuts, working only on the surface of the skin and placing stitches too far apart. "A few doctors," he cautioned, "even use clamps for such a facial wound. But for a young woman like this more care is necessary." He described how he had just finished suturing the deeper level and how it was time to begin the final, delicate work.

After a few moments he calmly pointed out his handiwork to me: "See how close together I'm making the stitches," he remarked. "There's a good medical reason for this. The closer together they are, the finer the scar. In fact, if you're especially careful, as I'm being, and administer the right antibiotic and dress the wound correctly, the scar will be so small that it won't even be noticed."

That got the young woman's attention. Then came the final pronouncement: "I think she'll be just as good as new!" There quickly appeared the hint of a smile on the girl's face.

Not bad for a country doctor who thought psychology was for the birds. Now, I thought, I can hit the sack.

FROM ON HIGH

When I was still single and in my mid-twenties my parents invited me to travel with them as they toured Great Britain and Ireland. It was a packaged tour for about thirty people covering fifteen days. I jumped at the chance since it was late summer and graduate school had not yet begun.

It was a beautiful day in Scotland: mid-seventies, blue sky, heather in full bloom. The bus had stopped for an afternoon break and we were all outside enjoying the weather and engaging in pleasantries. Mom and Dad were standing together talking with others from the tour. I was doing the same, standing close to them with Dad off to my side about three or four feet. I don't recall what my parents were discussing with their fellow travelers, but they were in good spirits and enjoying themselves. Little did they know what was about to happen.

It came "out of the blue"—literally. From the heavens, silently tumbling, gaining speed with each passing second, came the missile. Hurling through space, following Newton's various laws, it plunged. I'm sure that the attack was a random shot with no particular target in mind but, as fate would have it, something, someone, was in the wrong place at the wrong time.

Surprisingly, when it struck it made almost no sound. Just a little "splat." Its impact was quite soft too, for the target was unaware of having been hit.

I, however, witnessed the dastardly blow. So did two or three other travelers. Instinctively, we glanced toward the sky. Clearly seen, silhouetted against the blue sky, was the villain— an eagle circling far above. This handsome creature had dropped the offending lump earthward.

As I stared at this brown lump sitting so perfectly on my father's right shoulder, my mouth was frozen in the open position. I exhaled, trying to think of something to say. I also tried to keep from laughing.

"Dad," I finally managed to stammer, "I think you should take off your suit coat."

"Why?" he responded. "I'm not too warm. I'm comfortable."

"Dad, trust me," I repeated. "You really should remove your coat. There's something on your shoulder that you should know about."

He turned and looked. By now everyone around him was looking. Most were either covering up mouths with hands or smiling outright. (It's always funnier when eagles "attack" someone else!)

"Oh, sh——," someone uttered as I slid the jacket off my father's shoulder and arm. The perfect response, I thought, doubly so if you get my meaning. The source of this utterance? Lost in the commotion, or to history, if you get my point.

GET A HOLD OF YOURSELF

Few people realize it, but during my undergraduate days I functioned as a doctor, well, "medical student" might be a more accurate description. Though beginning college as a history major—and returning to this focus later—somewhere in the middle of my studies I switched to pre-med. Loyalty to my father played a role, but I also had a sincere interest in biology and things medical. I gave it a try, and for a few summers my life was filled with incredible experiences. For as soon as I switched, my father made me a part of his medical "team," joining his staff of nurses and the one other physician, Dr. Harry Wilbur, who cooperated with him at Smith Hospital. Just about everything was open to me, at his office in our home and at the hospital.

As I look back on those years now, I realize that in three brief summers I had more concrete medical adventures than most four-year medical students. (Today, given our changing world, this would be a very unlikely scenario.) I joined him as he stitched up numerous wounds, changed dressings to avoid infections, and examined patients for a variety of ailments. What impressed me most was how careful he was, how tenderly he would remove a dressing, for example, and gently replace it with a new one after applying just the right amount of antibiotic ointment. "Bob," I heard him say on more than one occasion, "there's no reason for infections to occur. If you do the job correctly, an infection can't develop." And infections never did seem to be an issue when he performed the work.

Some of my fondest memories, however, relate to my service as a young "surgeon," an assistant to my father when he operated at Smith Hospital. It was a weird and exhilarating feeling to be twenty years old and scrubbing up in anticipation of the morning's surgery! Normally this occurred when his associate was absent. So there would be only three of us—a nurse to administer the anesthetic, my father, and me.

Standing across from the head surgeon, I would follow his instructions and basically try to stay out of his way. Mostly it involved holding instruments and cutting suture when told to cut. Even this could be scary, though. More than once I would snip and he would snap in response, "Not so close!"

Standing across from him, and wishing I could massage my aching young back, I helped him remove tonsils and appendixes; gallbladders and pinning of broken hips were also a part of my overall experience, as was delivering babies, even one Caesarean.

In general, I would say that I performed "superbly" during these operations. All the patients recovered, that is, no one died because I forgot to remove a piece of gauze or because I cut too closely. My confidence soared to new heights.

That is not to say that everything was rosy. My most acute memory is of an operation that we performed in the summer of my senior year in college. By this time events had transpired to lead me away from medicine as a profession, though no final action had yet been taken. I think my father knew a little of my ambivalence but he hid his disappointment and said nothing.

Anyway, it was a miserably hot and humid August morning as the operation began. (Air conditioning was not a feature of this room, and fans were not recommended.) I recall that it was a gallbladder removal, though it may have been an appendix. Dad was his usual self, talking about everything except the procedure itself. (How surgeons do this and not lose concentration I still haven't figured out.) He was in fine spirits, but his assistant was having some "difficulty." I don't know whether it was skipping breakfast or eating something which was not setting right on my stomach or the oppressive heat and humidity, but something was wrong. I felt a little strange as the operating commenced and got progressively worse. I tried to move around a little, to bend and stretch, to breathe deeply. Nothing seemed to work. After about thirty minutes I knew I was in trouble. Big trouble!

Hot flashes suddenly occurred, rushing up from my stomach to my face. I realized that my forehead was sweating, that my heart was racing, and that the room was beginning to spin around somewhat. "Dad," I finally blurted out, "I'm not feeling so well."

"Don't worry," came the nonchalant response. "Every doctor feels a little sick from time to time during surgery."

I took a few more deep breaths, hoping I would return to normal. No luck. Within seconds I realized, in horror, that I wasn't going to make it; I was going to faint dead away, right in the middle of the operating room.

"Dad, it's not working; I think I'm going to faint," I managed weakly to say.

"Well, step back," came his immediate and stern response. "Whatever you do, don't faint on the patient! Step away, remove your mask, and lie down on your back. I'll finish here. It won't take long."

So there I was, on my back, staring up at the ceiling, trying not to pass out or lose my breakfast. Knowing that most doctors faced similar moments was of little comfort. I couldn't imagine this happening to my father—a man who claims he's never even had a headache. It was humbling, humiliating. That was the last time I ever operated with my father.

HOUSE CALL

It was about 1:30 p.m. when the call came. The request was a familiar one: Would the doctor be able to make a house call in the country, about five miles from home? The voice seemed a little apologetic, questioning if this part of his general practice had long since been abandoned. Even I wondered what he would say, since house calls were by then, in fact, quite rare.

I didn't have long to wait, for upon replacing the phone he turned to me and queried: "How would you like to drive me out into the country? It won't take long. There's an old woman who's declining and needs some attention."

"But Dad," I responded, "surely one of the other doctors in town could make the trip?"

"They can't find one," he replied matter-of-factly. "Besides, these young men charge too much money for a house call. I believe it's now fifty dollars. That's a little too much, don't you think?" I did.

So I drove him out into the countryside, along a winding road, first past newer homes, then past older farms. It was September, and the leaves were already turning. The feel and smell of autumn was in the air. It was a beautiful day. So many memories rushed in upon me—of similar trips, in days gone by, throughout greater Walton and Delaware County. It all seemed like yesterday to me then, during those brief minutes, so comforting, so right.

We found the house and parked the car. I helped him with the bigger of his two bags. Before we walked to the house, though, I made him stop and let me "catch" him with my trusty camera. Only upon reviewing this scene later in the day did I realize how special it was. Not only did the video reveal this veteran GP walking carefully along the stone steps, but it captured the color of the turning leaves and the sight of cows grazing in a field across the road. Truly a country house call!

Once inside the house it seemed like a homecoming. He remembered a little about the house—who had lived there in previous years—and became reacquainted with the son and daughter-in-law of the elderly woman. They had both been his patients some time ago; in fact, Dad had removed the man's appendix in the 1950s. (Proving that Dad is only human, he had only a dim memory of this operation.)

I filmed him from time to time as he displayed his unique bedside manner. He talked to the woman, who was unresponsive. He talked mainly to the family, but not just about the patient. Everything seemed to interest him. He described some of the medical changes that had occurred during his years of practice; he mentioned some of his activities related to the Eells Family Association—hard to silence him long about that topic. Politics, the weather, the daughter-in-law's arthritis: many subjects surfaced as he kept up a steady flow of words. The relatives were quite pleased with this type of banter, interacting with the doctor, making it seem like he was a concerned neighbor stopping by to offer advice. The son even remembered some "ancient" history—my own days as a high school basketball player for Walton Central.

The elderly woman, though, the primary purpose of the visit, was indeed failing. She was very weak and made only the slightest response to the doctor's questions. She had stopped eating and existed primarily on tea and broth. The son noted that she had been in the hospital a few years back and hated the experience. She would rather die than return to that environment, she had told her son. It did appear that she wanted to die and that she wanted to do so at home, surrounded by family and friends.

The doctor didn't have very much to suggest except that they try to get her to take more food, especially solids. "Some older folks just give up," he said with resignation. "Perhaps at eighty-eight that's what she's telling us and we have to listen." He did go on to suggest a few more practical steps to initiate, including getting a county nurse to stop by and set up a schedule of visits.

The relatives appeared to agree substantially with the diagnosis and thanked the doctor for his willingness to make the trip out on such short notice. The son paid him in cash, and it was considerably less than fifty dollars.

Before we departed, though, I had to say something upbeat and encouraging. I was a little anxious because I wasn't sure how the family would respond. But I screwed up my courage and took the plunge. I pulled aside the younger woman and gave her this piece of advice: "After we leave, at an appropriate moment, why not tell your mom that eighty-eight is not really that 'old.' There are plenty of people older than she who are still going strong. In fact, the loquacious doctor who just paid her a visit is older than she is. He recently celebrated his ninetieth birthday and still has plenty to keep him going!"

By the look on her face, I knew it would be done.

SNAPSHOTS

Of Walter and Katherine Eells
There are so many stories and memories. Here are just a few...

My mother remembers once when a meal was interrupted by anxious parents who rushed into the office with a daughter in their arms—blue from a blocked air passage. Nothing they had done had worked. My father quickly took the child into the examining room and flashed a light down the throat. He could see nothing, but something was obviously stuck and there was little time to act. By now the parents were on the verge of hysteria. So, he did what a country doctor would do, hoping it would work: he put his hand down her throat as far as possible, extended his index finger even farther, probed and hooked the object, and pulled it free. Within seconds the child was breathing regularly and her color had returned to normal. Today the Heimlich maneuver would no doubt be used. Father's, however, was just as effective.

* * * *

My pre-med days would have been incomplete, thought my Dad, without at least one autopsy. So one afternoon I joined him in the examining room of a local funeral home. My memories are quite vivid: of the sights and smells of the corpse and of the whole environment. Dad, of course, was interested in all the details, showing me the vital organs and pointing out the trouble spots which had contributed to the death. But even he was uncomfortable with the experience, since cancer had been the principal culprit and the smell of the opened body was not pleasant. I remember well this comment: "I prefer poking around in live specimens and making them well again. Don't you think that's preferable, Bob?" I certainly did.

* * * * *

One of the most humorous episodes, at least in retrospect, occurred one day when Dad called me across the street to the hospital to help him examine and treat several minor injuries suffered by three people in a car accident. We treated the two adults first and then turned to the final passenger—an attractive young woman about my age, maybe nineteen or twenty. She winced from a few scrapes and bruises but held up well during the application of antibiotics and the bandages. When the procedures were apparently completed, my father asked if she hurt anywhere else. She responded that her upper leg and hip hurt a little, causing a slight limp. The jeans weren't torn, but an examination was necessary, according to the doctor. So without a second thought, he asked him to remove her jeans. My heart rate increased a little as I wondered what would come next. She hesitated, looked first at Dad, then at me, then back to Dad again. It took a few seconds before Dad realized what was happening. Then he said calmly and confidently, "It's all right, he's going to be a doctor." Her hesitation ended and down came her jeans. My heart rate increased even more.

* * * *

Not even a brief tribute to this country doctor would be complete without a review of some of his remarkable medical accomplishments. Dad, for example, was one of the first doctors in Delaware County to use the new experimental drug, penicillin. Through a U.S. Army contact in Boston during World War II, he received a few ounces of a rather crude, early version of the penicillin drug. Crude but effective, he told me, since it worked: first on a young man with a serious infection, then on many others with a multitude of bacterial invasions, including syphilis. Syphilis, by the way, had been previously treated by him and others with a form of arsenic.

Among his proudest achievements are his "deliveries": helping to bring about 2100 babies into the world. The bottom floor of Smith Hospital had been converted over the years into the maternity section, and most of the children were born there. But many, as you might expect, were born at home, as this country doctor would arrive in the nick of time. Several Walton families even had the good fortune of having Dr. Eells deliver three generations of babies!

Many hundreds of operations were performed by this GP at Smith and Delaware Valley Hospitals, as well as elsewhere. He performed a great many appendectomies and pinned a lot of hips. He especially remembers that he and a colleague performed thirteen tonsillectomies in one day, for which they were paid $12.50 each per operation.

Some day someone needs to make a tabulation of all such accomplishments. And this would be possible to do, since Dad has carefully retained all of his scheduling books from his many years of practice-—sixty-two as of now and still counting.

* * * * *

To say that I grew up in a medical family is an understatement. It's not just that my father worked twelve to sixteen hours a day, six (sometimes seven) days a week, and rarely took a vacation (except to take me to college—a brief respite). More needs to be said. His office was (and still is) in our house at 35 Townsend Street. It consisted of four rooms, not including a medicine closet and a bathroom. The waiting room opened directly into our dining room, making family privacy difficult to guard. My memories are that it was almost always full of patients, most of the day and well into the night. Twenty to thirty people would wait to be examined on a typical day. Many patients would talk to me or my brother or sister or to Mom as we passed by the usually open door. The friendlier ones would walk right into the dining room to strike up a conversation.

26

The office also contained a room with Dad's desk and files, an examining room, and a laboratory—where blood and urine samples were tested and shots were normally administered. It was in this lab that I was trained to run simple tests and where I learned to hate the smell of a boiling-needle-gone-dry. It still turns my nose and turns over my stomach to this day.

Smith Hospital, named for Dad's stepfather, and where his mother served as a nurse for many years, was directly across the street, not 75 feet from our house. So even when Dad wasn't in the house or office, he was still involved in medicine, a few feet away, making rounds or operating. It served as a hospital for over thirty years, then became a nursing home for a few more years, before he sold it so that it could continue as a boarding home for the elderly. When it was a hospital, Smith was as warm and friendly as any such institution ever gets. When the state closed it down because it was an older, wooden structure, many patients and friends were upset; when the nursing home was terminated subsequently, some patients wept.

One of my fondest memories, however, about Smith Hospital has little to do with medicine. It's related to food—rich, tasty, nourishing food—served in large quantities in the kitchen by Mrs. Northrup to any doctor's son who happened to be in the area. And that was me. Frequently.

* * * * *

I don't remember the exact context, but somehow in the late 1950s a connection was made by Jefferson Medical School in Philadelphia with my father. As a result, four different medical students spent summers with Dad, learning about the trials and joys of general practice. And brother, did they ever learn! Each one had barely unpacked before being ushered into the world of a country doctor. A vacation, it was not. But I don't recall any of them complaining. A full immersion is what they wanted and what they received.

It makes me smile to reflect upon those summers, seeing the "summer interns" following Dad around, soaking up all those experiences. Dad, of course, was in his element. He wouldn't have been very good at formal lecturing; hands-on practical exposure, however, was his teaching forte. He loved every minute of it. I don't know why the interns stopped coming. Maybe the rumor arose that he worked them to death. At any rate, Dad could have gone on for years. And those young men who lived this kind of medicine were a privileged few. One intern, upon leaving, told me that he had learned more during the summer than in all of his formal classes combined. No doubt.

* * * * *

Dad's busy schedule was stressful. Apart from reading historical novels and watching a few television shows (e.g., "Hogan's Heroes"), he never learned to slow down and relax much. He was also, obviously, a perfectionist, which further increased the level of stress in his life. Thus those individuals, for example, who could not meet his high standards bothered him immensely. He never said much to them directly, but he muttered to me and other family members about their slackness and carelessness. Even such a seemingly insignificant thing as having a nurse or nurse's aide bang a bed against a wall, chipping the paint, really disturbed him. (It didn't thrill me, either, since I was usually the one assigned to repaint those spots.)

We all respond to stress differently. Dad's physiological response was painful—for him to suffer and for others to watch. Canker sores were his manifestation of stress. He always seemed to have them in his mouth: big, white spots that looked awful and no doubt felt even worse than they looked. I would watch him trying to eat, shifting food from the offending side of his mouth to the clear side, chewing and swallowing with difficulty. It was not a pleasant sight. Maybe that's why he was prone to eat rapidly, swallowing in big gulps. Not the best strategy in terms of family politics, but it certainly shortened the period of physical agony.

Amazingly, when Dad was away from his office for even two or three days (long for him), the sores disappeared. He could taste food again and eat normally. Unfortunately, they returned within days back in Walton. No medicine worked very well to inhibit them or relieve the pain. He just learned to live with it. Had he been given the choice between switching professions and being free of this burden and continuing his non-stop medical career, we all know what choice he would have made.

* * * * *

The phone was another source of stress in the Eells family. We had several outlets but only one number. When it rang it did so throughout the house. And it rang most of the day and much of the night. It was also set at the highest decibel level so that only the dead could avoid its jarring call for attention.

During the day we had help—nurses and secretaries to answer phones. Nighttime, however, was another story. It was Mom to the rescue.

Mother would be the receptionist, answering the phone during after-dinner office hours. Dad was usually too busy with patients anyway. Then later, after the last patient had departed, she would still be in charge. In fact, when the sound shattered the quiet of the early morning, as it frequently did, Mom usually took control. A typical scenario went like this: 1) phone rings at 2 a.m.; 2) Dad answers, since it is on his side of the bed; 3) Dad gets annoyed, since many callers had been "sick" for a day or two already; 4) Mom reaches over and takes the phone from Dad, trying to calm him down and being pleasant to the caller at the same time; 5) Mom says, "She really wants to be seen now and she sounds horrible. Can't you see her briefly?" 6) Unpleasantry from Dad; 7) "Walter," she whispers with her hand over the mouthpiece, "lower your voice, she can hear you"; 8)

Awkward silence; 9) Dad mutters, "All right, tell her to come in. I'll see her as soon as I can get dressed." Maybe it was also a case of Mom "rescuing" the patient.

* * * * *

Mom was truly amazing, being Dad's helper in so many ways. She answered phones, relayed a zillion messages, talked to patients—calming down the excited and encouraging the depressed; she even learned to perform a few simple procedures in the laboratory. Dad's all-consuming medical practice would never have been possible without her valuable assistance.

Let me provide just one example of her importance. Somewhere in the middle years of their teamwork, she became Dad's (and the family's) chauffeur. Driving him all over kingdom-come became one of her chief responsibilities. Dad didn't object to his being relegated to the shotgun position. He seemed to realize that it was for the best, and he was right. I remember more than once cringing as I watched him back the car out of our driveway into busy Townsend Street traffic. He never gave more than a glance at the potential traffic coming from either direction. I recall saying once, "Dad, you're going to get clobbered one day if you're not more careful." He just shrugged, not appearing to be bothered much by this impending disaster.

So Mom came to the rescue here, too.

* * * * *

In some respects, Mom was the spiritual force in the family. Dad's faith was quietly expressed, not the case with his partner. I remember taking part in family devotions in the morning, and I still hear them singing a psalm before breakfast when I visit my hometown. (Actually, I hear Mom singing and Dad doing something not quite so musical.)

Mother was a cornerstone for many decades in the Christian education program of the Walton Reformed Presbyterian Church, teaching several different Bible classes for young people. She gave leadership to the summer vacation Bible school programs and taught for many years in the "released-time" activities of the local public school. As a result, she became quite knowledgeable in Bible history and Reformed doctrine.

I also remember the amusing dynamics of Mom and Dad at the weekly Sunday morning church services: When the congregation had finished singing the last Psalm before the sermon, Dad would sit down and usually start to "nod off," at least to the casual observer. Actually, he didn't miss much, but you couldn't tell by his posture. Mom, of course, would gently nudge him in the side with her elbow, trying to guide his head back up a little. Sometimes it worked, sometimes not. They both seemed to approach this recurring phenomenon with the appropriate sense of humor.

* * * * *

Mom's nudging took many forms. Another humorous example happened in the mid-1960s. One day, tired of frequently driving to Beaver Falls, Pennsylvania, to visit my sister and me, and weary of Dad's "fear of flying," she took action. She called the local travel agent and reserved two tickets on a flight from Binghamton to Pittsburgh. No discussion had taken place; she simply did it.

On the day of departure, she packed the bags and declared that this time they would be flying. Flying!? I have no idea of Dad's precise response but, probably, momentary panic set in. Then he perhaps glanced at the bags and at the woman and headed for the car, a car pointed toward the airport.

Well, that's all it took to transform their lives. From that moment on they became world travelers, literally. They've traveled just about everywhere. Planes are like home to Dad now. He enters, sits down, puts a toothpick in his mouth, opens up his latest historical novel, and hardly even notices when the plane departs or lands.

See what a determined woman can accomplish, even with a stubborn Eells?

* * * * *

Mom has made an additional valuable contribution to the Eells and Henderson families, namely, by producing an extensive diary of events. Rarely has a daily entry been missed. She has, in fact, functioned as an amateur historian all these years. (It's nice to know that record-keeping has been done in a more systematic way than my own recollections.) Someday, someone will find her accounts very helpful in painting a more complete picture of two families and a fuller portrait of a remarkable couple.

* * * * *

What a unique couple they have been all these years. While outwardly rather shy, especially Dad, one would never know it in terms of how they have managed their household. You are familiar by now with some of the commotion that reigned there because of Dad's medical practice. But that's only a fraction of the wonderful, frenetic life witnessed at 35 Townsend Street. For, in a nutshell, their house became somewhat of a "motel," a friendly place of repose for all sorts of nomads: close family, Eells family connections, people associated with the Reformed Presbyterian Church, et al. Many visitors passed through this home, all warmly greeted and cared for by this "retiring" couple. Sometimes I was overwhelmed by clutter and noise; it was too much to handle—patients, visitors, ringing phones, two high-strung barking Schnauzers, etc. I would have to take a walk or go jogging just to calm my nerves.

Mom and Dad, on the other hand, seemed to thrive on all this activity. Maybe their famous, ostensible shyness all these years has been a clever disguise, a ploy to fill up their lives with human contact. If so, it has worked.

* * * * *

Mr. and Mrs. Scrabble is what they should be called, for SCRABBLE has been and continues to be their principal form of entertainment. When I called home recently, I interrupted the most recent game. It made me laugh and brought back many memories: of past games, of Dad's grasp of the English language and his amazing "luck," of the incredible variety of people this couple continues to entice into friendly competition. Even now, they continue to play two or three times a week, competing against, for example, a twenty-year-old neighbor, or their accountant, or a retired school teacher, or a visitor or two who are spending the night at the Eells "Motel." They sit around the card table, the TV remains on, the phone occasionally rings; Mom serves coffee and munchies, and Dad gets to play the "X" and the "Q and U" combination—in a triple letter or triple word fashion. I know of what I speak, since it happened to me during my last visit. Thus, be warned! If you visit, SCRABBLE is coming your way. And don't try to peruse the dictionary in search of words. The house rules are strictly enforced.

* * * * *

Another familiar sight in Walton is Dr. and Mrs. Eells visiting restaurants for the evening meal. Well, actually a particular restaurant, since they have a favorite on Main Street. It's a simple place, nothing fancy, where tasty "home cooking" is provided, according to Mom.

They usually arrive around 6 p.m., after the TV news, choose their favorite place beside a window, and place an order for the main meal. I use the singular because it is always one order. The waitress needs no special instructions. She prepares the order, bringing two plates with her on which she places identical portions. Nourishing food is then consumed and greetings made to others in the room. Rarely is anyone ignored.

In retrospect, I think this is one of my parents' most endearing qualities to the people of Walton. This "ordinary" place suits them fine. They don't drive twenty miles to a plush restaurant in the belief that Main Street options are beneath them. They're not snobbish; they're very loyal to Walton businesses and to the people of that "ordinary" town. You can tell that it is appreciated.

* * * * *

In a more serious vein, Dad's financial generosity has been exemplary. And I don't mean just with his children and immediate family members. He has been generous in his contributions to churches, colleges and universities, and charities of all kinds. Individuals too have frequently received his support. Whether it was a college student who needed tuition assistance, a Waltonian who sought aid for his business, or a couple with mounting medical bills, all have received his support.

When I was about ten years old, something unusual—even for the Eells family—occurred. It was about 8:00 p.m. and already dark. The entire family was in the living room watching TV. Someone knocked on the front door, not the office door which would have been normal. Dad turned on the porch light and opened the door. A man appeared before him, disheveled and speaking softly. Dad stepped outside to continue the conversation. I, of course, crossed over to the door which had remained slightly ajar. The stranger wanted money, I heard him say. He seemed embarrassed to be asking, even while calling it a loan. They talked for a minute or two, then Dad brought him into the house and left the room briefly. Now everyone was embarrassed. When Dad returned he ushered the man back outside and placed something in his hand. That was it. Dad re-entered and closed the door. "He was a little short this month and needed some help," declared Dad quietly. We all returned to our "normal" evening. It was, though, very quiet in the room for a few minutes.

* * * * *

Somehow Dad managed also to be generous with his community service. In particular I am thinking of his twenty-plus years on the boards of the Ogden Free Library, the Walton Central School, and the vocational school, BOCES. The latter honored him several years ago by naming one structure the Walter E. Eells Building. Dad has never been one to brag about his accomplishments but is justly proud of this award, pointing it out to family and friends when driving past the vocational complex. It's nice to be reminded that this building will be around for many years to come.

* * * * *

All children give their parents tough moments and happy ones. That was certainly true of Eleanor, Bob, and Ken. Some favorite memories of my own gift of happiness, though, relate to my years of sports activity, especially basketball at the high school. Athletics was never a part of my father's life, perhaps a little less true of my mother's. But they both began to live a pretty rich, vicarious life of competitive sports when I reached the ninth grade.

For the next four years, as I recall, neither parent missed a basketball game, home or away—seventy-three games as I make the tally. I started every game and played a ton of minutes, so they had many reasons to cheer, groan, and gasp. I mention the latter because of my "wild" ways on the court. I dove for every loose ball on the floor, flew through the air to keep balls in play (usually managing to land in the lap of a surprised cheerleader), and raced up the court to score an easy lay-up.

Sometimes I gave them a real scare. I remember one close game where we managed to come from behind and with a few seconds remaining trailed by only two points. A teammate swiped the ball, and I sprinted down the court to receive the lead pass. I got it, jumped, and shot—just as a defensive player plowed into me with a full head of steam. The shot was successful and the noise was deafening, but I was thrown into the unprotected concrete wall of the gym. I bounced off the wall and rolled back onto the court, a little dizzy but mostly just milking the moment for all it was worth. The gym was very quiet for a few seconds as the coach and players rushed to see if I was still alive. As I sat up I glanced at my parents in the bleachers. Alarm etched Mom's face; even Dad's normally more impassive face showed concern. I didn't feel too guilty until later for I had to step to the foul line and sink the winning penalty shot—which I did. Then smiles etched both of their faces.

Mostly, though, I remember the other moments, glances stolen in the heat of battle, when my performance on the court brought them so much pleasure. I cherish those memories.

* * * * *

Here are a few final snapshots: Dad at his desk, calling on the phone and talking for many minutes. A lively conversation. Dad typing a letter with his own two fingers or dictating to his secretary. Dad perusing a large green volume on his desk, fascinated with the details. Dad editing a manuscript and having Mom rush it over to the post office because it's already overdue at the printer. Dad talking about one particular subject, especially to family members, until the eyes of the listener cross and the ears plug up, failing to keep pace.

I've been describing my father, not involved in the medicine he loves, but caught up in something he has come, in the last decade, to love just as much—everything having to do with the Eells Family Association. He's the editor of the family bulletin, the family's principal historian, "host" of the annual reunion, and "cheerleader" *extraordinaire* of family business.

Eells is a name he carries proudly.

Robert J. Eells

Part II

Essays and Comments from

COUNTRY DOCTOR

Second Edition (1994)

Dedicated to the memory of my brother,
Kenneth E. Eells

Robert J. Eells

YOU FIRST

What will it be this time, wondered the young doctor as his colleague drove them toward the origin of the desperate call? "Please hurry," the woman had yelled into the phone, "my husband is having convulsions on the front porch. I can't restrain him, and they won't stop!"

Funny about life in a small town. Just about anything can happen, medically or otherwise. This truth was about to explode in the face of Dr. Eells—once again.

Upon arriving, the two doctors rushed up onto the porch and were, indeed, confronted by a man whose arms and legs were thrashing the air in all directions. His head, too, was jerking up and down, though his wife was able to keep it from smashing into the wooden floor of the porch. It was at the other end, however, that Dad's attention was initially focused. The man's legs were thrusting up and then crashing down upon a low railing located at the end of the porch. Each time they were hitting the area of the Achilles heel, increasing the possibility of rupturing these tissues so important to human motion. Dad's first action, therefore, was to push the legs away from the railing. Total restraint was made easier not only by the presence of two additional people at the scene, but also by the rapid administering of a sedative carried in Dr. Eells' always-available "black bag."

The patient was transported back to Smith Hospital where careful examination began into the cause of the violent seizure. The seriousness of the situation was confirmed by the man's vital signs—blood pressure, heart rate, pupil dilation—which were all weak or abnormal.

Doc Eells feared brain damage—tumor or blood clot and began setting up the x-ray machine. This was the mid-1930s and the equipment was primitive by today's standards, but that's all they had to work with. As they waited for the film to develop, they pondered two possibilities: one where the film was inconclusive, the other where "something" did appear, but concerning which they had few medical options at their disposal.

"Well," sighed Dad, pointing to the x-ray, "there it is." And there it was, a definite spot on the film that was no doubt a major part of the problem. But was it a tumor or a blood clot? After consulting, the two young doctors decided it was the latter, but even this "lesser" condition was troublesome. What could be done about this large clot located at the base of the skull? Could it be reduced by drugs? Not likely, and besides it appeared that time was of the essence.

The other doctor was stumped. Dad, though, was pacing the floor, deep in thought. "Got any ideas?" came the query from his colleague. "Yes," came the nervous reply, "but it's a little risky." Risky was an understatement.

Briefly, Dad related a true story that had happened to him during his internship in a Binghamton hospital. A similar situation had occurred at a time when he was set to observe a medical procedure by one of his professors. "Today," the surgeon had said, "you're in for a real treat." The professor then explained that an emergency had just developed involving a man with a large blood clot at the base of his skull, and surgery was the only real choice. The patient was brought in and prepped. As this was taking place, the surgeon described the very delicate nature of the operation, how the blood would be withdrawn through a needle placed in precisely the right position. He went on to point out that the needle had to be placed between the correct two vertebrae and must not waver up or down, left or right, even slightly. A mistake in either the position or the steadiness would result in death or permanent paralysis. The operation took place before a fascinated audience.

Dad stopped recounting the story and asked, "What do you think; want to give it a try?" His colleague didn't believe that they had much choice, but looked a little pale. "You'll do it, though?" he asked expectantly. "I mean, I'd be more comfortable if you initiated the actual procedure." Then he hesitated and thought of one more question: "Walter, you didn't finish the story; what happened to the patient whose operation you witnessed?"

Silence. Biting his lip, Doc Eells finally replied: "He died. The professor had been drinking and I guess his hands weren't steady enough." Dad's colleague became even more pale.

Well, Dad found the right spot, with a steady hand, and the blood was withdrawn. "Now," he concluded, "all we can do is wait." A few hours later the patient regained consciousness. Slowly, he returned to a normal life. And he lived for many, many years.

General practice isn't what it used to be.

JUST DESSERT

I was a terrible tease. I made life uncomfortable for many people—kidding around, joking, punning, mocking, doing whatever was necessary to divert attention away from my insecure self toward some other hapless soul. Sometimes it really was funny and harmless. At times it was quite awkward, like when I teased the very young women whom I found attractive, but didn't have the courage to date. At other times it was cruel and thoughtless. But even then, life had a way of straightening things out.

For example...I had the habit of teasing my younger brother, Ken, about a certain physical trait of his. Ken was always on the diminutive side, even at full development several inches shorter and usually 20-30 pounds lighter than myself. That alone probably wouldn't have punched my tease button much, but something else did: namely, the area just above his beltline. During his early adolescence, Ken had developed a little extra flesh around his lower abdomen, what is usually called a "spare tire" in older men. Of course, it didn't take brother Bob long to discover this flaw and to exploit it to the fullest.

I quickly came to call it his "roll" and him "rolly." Hardly a day transpired without me using one label or another. A favorite time of the day for me was dinner, when I would invariably ask my brother to "pass the rolls." And verbal assault wasn't my only weapon. I would also pull a "Pearl Harbor," diving in and grabbing his spare tire whenever he let down his guard for a moment. Nice guy, huh? Not to Ken, naturally. To him, the situation contained <u>no</u> humor.

One day, however, the pendulum swung back, so to speak. Ken and I were taking a break in mid-afternoon, having a reasonably good time as I recall. We were in the kitchen; the snacks were going down fine; life was great in the Eells household. Mom was around and Dad had come in once or twice from the office, but they were minor players in the unfolding melodrama. I

46

don't know what came over me but something made me ruin this pastoral scene by uttering the hated phrase, "Mom, can we have any 'rolls' with the ice cream and cookies?" Silence from Ken, and the same from Mom, except I turned around to catch a scowl on her face after the question had been asked. I kept this up for a few seconds, during which time Dad also re-entered the kitchen. He realized what was going on and didn't look too thrilled, either.

It happened just as I was turning back toward the table to continue the tormenting of my brother. In a flash Ken had picked up his bowl of ice cream and delivered a perfect right cross, not a hook or an uppercut, but a precise, short knockout punch—right into my face! Up my nose it went and even into my mouth, since I had just started to deliver my next line. Ken held the bowl there for a brief instant, then let it drop into my lap. He rose, burped a short laugh, cracked a wicked smile and bolted from the room.

I was, of course, both stunned and outraged. I froze, not from the ice cream, but from the shock and the indignity. I exhaled, spraying droplets across the table and onto the picture window. Then I screamed bloody murder in the direction of my departed brother. I turned back to my parents for sympathy, if not empathy, but to no avail. I started the "protest of the innocent" but was cut short by a terse comment from one of my parents (I can't even remember which one): "You deserved it, Bob." And I did. I really did.

I just wish that I had Ken back today to do it again. And again..., teaching me whatever lesson he felt necessary.

YOU'RE KIDDING ME?

There once was a woman named Ruth who told a wonderful (true) story. It goes something like this...

Ruth had been a patient of Doc Eells years ago. She had visited him several times in his office for a variety of medical reasons, and he had, of course, also made a few house calls over the years. The doctor had also delivered her daughter. He was truly her family physician.

As an elderly woman, though, she had moved to Florida and was rarely in contact with the Eells family—a short written note once in awhile was the only communication. This woman's daughter, too, had scattered to the winds, living for some time in crowded southern California.

As it happens, Ruth enjoyed visiting the daughter in California and was encamped there about two years ago when something amazing took place: One day Ruth and her daughter were talking shop when they were interrupted by the doorbell. The cleaning woman had arrived to do her weekly chores. Nothing unusual about this. But as she was dusting around the living room she kept glancing down at the coffee table at a newspaper which had recently been placed there.

Again, nothing too unusual, except that it wasn't a local paper, or even a California paper, but the <u>Oneonta Star</u>, a small daily newspaper published in Oneonta, New York. What, thought the two other women, would be so fascinating to the cleaning woman in this far-away paper? They didn't say anything, but continued to be amused by the situation.

Finally, the visitor stopped cleaning and asked if she could read the story (with picture) on the page in front of her. "Sure," came the response from the daughter, "be my guest." Well, the cleaning woman finally finished the story and then paused with a funny look on her face. Intrigued, Ruth broke the silence with a question: "I see that you were reading the story about the recent retirement of Dr. Walter Eells. I'm curious. Do you know this doctor?"

"If he's the Dr. Eells of Walton, New York—as it appears from the article—I certainly do know him. Or remember him. About forty years ago he saved my brother's life!"

"He what?" came the incredulous response from Ruth.

Again. "He saved my brother's life!" Then the story unfolded. When this woman had been a young girl living in Bloomville, New York, her three-month old brother, Donald, had become seriously ill. The county nurse had suggested that the parents take the child to Walton to be under the care of Dr. Eells, in whom she apparently had great confidence. The parents followed her advice. They did, indeed, travel to Walton, where the infant was admitted into Smith Hospital.

"What happened to your brother?" asked the daughter. "Well, he recovered and lived many healthy years," came the thankful response. The women then marveled at what a small world it really is. Really.

Dad, as it turns out, learned of this story from Ruth Ewing herself, who related it to him in a letter. Checking the Smith Hospital records, he subsequently found an infant named Donald Jacobs who had been admitted into Smith Hospital in 1938, with erysipelas. He concluded matter-of-factly: "I suspect I prescribed some sulpha drug and he cleared up and didn't come back."

Delaware County, New York, Florida, California; it seems like Dad's impact has been far flung, doesn't it?

DON'T MOVE!

The woman entered Dad's office just at the close of evening office hours, around 10:30 p.m. She was pregnant, very pregnant, and had previously called to complain about some suspicious pain she had been experiencing. At Dad's suggestion she had decided to hurry over for a quick check up, just in case.

Since she was not due to deliver for a few weeks, Dad spent a couple of minutes finishing some paperwork before turning his attention to his final patient of another long day and night. "Have you been having any contractions?" Dad inquired as he was taking her blood pressure. She responded that she had been having occasional pains, but didn't know whether or not to call them contractions. Dad pondered this answer for a few moments, but since her signs appeared relatively normal, he wasn't overly concerned.

Abruptly, the woman announced that she had to use the bathroom. Not unusual for her situation, so Dad wasn't alarmed. A few minutes later, though, when sounds of discomfort emanated from the bathroom, the Doctor called out: "Everything O.K. in there?"

"I feel kind of funny," came the shaky response. "Maybe I should come out and lie down for a little while."

"Fine," said the doctor, "just use the examining table in the next room."

She opened the door, took two or three steps, and stopped— holding onto the back of the nearest chair for support. When she spoke, the hair on the back of Dad's neck quickly stood at full attention. "Doc," she blurted out, "something's wrong. I think I'm having the baby right now!" Time seemed to stand still.

"Let's get you up onto the table," came the command from Dad after a few suspenseful seconds. He put his arm under her elbow and started to lead her toward the table. The unborn child, however, didn't seem to care about orders from a doctor. He had other plans; he wanted to be born on his own schedule.

50

So, the woman stopped again, and with a look of panic, yelled, "It's coming now doctor, right now, I can feel it!" Glancing at the floor, the doctor saw confirmation of the imminent event: a puddle of amniotic fluid.

"Stop right here," ordered my father and spread your legs so that I can see what's going on." He proceeded to fall to his knees and lift up the woman's skirt, showing little concern for this otherwise delicate situation.

At that very instant the baby dropped, right into the outstretched hands of the surprised country doctor! "I got him," exclaimed my Dad, confidently, knowing of course how closely they had come to having the baby crash head first onto the floor. The doctor then helped the mother into the chair and placed the newborn infant upon her lap. They both stared at the healthy, crying baby for a few seconds, then at each other. Smiles appeared on both their faces, especially Dad's. "It's not every day," he laughed, "that I deliver a baby in this manner." No joke.

But, if you did give birth like that woman, you would indeed want someone around like Doc Eells.

MEMORIES

January 1907. The shades were being drawn, the voices lowered, and the little boy—barely four years old—was once again nervous. Mommy had been sick the first time, sick for what seemed a long time. Everyone had whispered and tipped-toed around the house waiting on Mommy.

Now it was happening again: The darkened house, the whispers, the neighbors coming over with food—he liked that part. Overall, though, it was scary. This time it was Mommy who was in charge, taking care of him and his little sister, Evelyn, and big brother, Ben. And Mommy was also nursing her special patient in her bedroom. He was a little confused about who was sick this time. Big brother said it was Daddy. Daddy?

The next morning Mommy was hard on them—speaking sharply about being more quiet with their games and playing. In the afternoon the man with the black bag returned and spent some time with her and the special patient. Finally, he came out, speaking quietly to Mommy and glancing occasionally across the room toward the children. She walked the man to the door and thanked him for his help. But then she stopped and just looked out the front window for a few moments. Was Mommy crying?

Then she turned and walked toward them. "Children," she said, "your father would like to speak with you, one at a time." When it was his turn the middle child obediently followed his mother into the darkened bedroom. The room smelled funny, like medicine. He just stood awkwardly at the foot of the bed, not knowing what to do.

"Son," came a weak voice from the bed. "Come up by me. Sit here beside me on the bed." He did as he was told and climbed up. His brother was right: it was his Daddy. His Daddy looked pale and seemed to fight just to smile. Later, he wouldn't remember much of what his father said to him, only that he spoke softly and offered a brief prayer. Then he climbed down and it was little sister's turn.

That little boy, so long ago, was Walter Eells. The sick man was, indeed, his father, Clarence. He was on his death bed. Pneumonia. This is the only real memory my father has of my grandfather. Clarence had nursed his wife, Carrie, back to health, but had also caught her disease. She survived; he didn't. (There weren't any antibiotics in those days.) Maybe, as the years unfolded, this event was one of the reasons why the young Walter decided that medicine was in his future.

KIDS SAY THE DARNDEST THINGS

In the first edition I included a funny story about a child who didn't like getting a shot from Doc Eells. Well, he's not the only one who objected; many have done so, in fact, yours truly had such an experience. And funny isn't quite the word I would use to describe it.

I remember that one evening I was watching TV in the living room in early fall. My homework must have been finished, since I usually wasn't allowed this privilege unless assignments were completed. I must have been about eleven or twelve years old. Old enough, I thought, to make up my own mind about important subjects.

I was glued to the set and enjoying myself when Mom appeared in the room. "Bob," she calmly interrupted, "do you remember that Dad has to give you your school shot tonight?" Naturally, this fact had somehow slipped my mind. "Oh," I gulped, "does it have to be tonight?" She repeated tonight was it and that Dad would shortly be ready, as soon as the last patient departed from the office.

Before I could think of an escape plan or even an excuse, Dad appeared out of nowhere with a needle in his hand! "Do you want to get it here or in the office?" he asked. Neither, I thought to myself in panic. I stood up and something inside me just snapped. I started to backpedal and move toward the front stairs.

"Oh no you don't," he blurted out as he headed toward me. "You've had shots before. They don't hurt much at all."

Easy for him to say, I thought. The chase began. I ran up the front stairs, down the hallway, and down the back stairs, making a full circle in a flash. In fact, I circled the house twice, though Dad probably thought it was more like ten times. Soon, though, his better half intervened: heading up for the third time, Mom blocked my path and I was trapped—like a rat as the saying goes.

Dad grabbed my arm, wiped it with the alcohol swab, and started the movement for injection. I snapped again.

"Damn it! I hate you, I hate you," I screamed just before the inevitable happened. He paused, no doubt a little shocked, and then thrust the needle into my arm. Perhaps somewhat more forcefully than would have otherwise been the case, or at least it seemed to me.

It wasn't over. I jumped up and with great indignity screamed pretty much the same words again. (There's nothing like an indignant rat.) Dad gave me the same look—a mixture of sadness and anger. I ran down the stairs, threw open the front door, and charged out in the night, feeling more sorry for myself than physical pain.

Within a few seconds, of course, I felt the appropriate degree of shame and guilt. It was a silly and hurtful thing to say. I knew even then, though, that neither Dad nor Mom really believed the words. But, on the other hand, I don't recall ever apologizing. Probably I was too embarrassed.

Well, I didn't mean it Dad.

Now, I've come clean.

Robert J. Eells

THE WORLD'S GREATEST PHYSICIAN

I've always enjoyed listening to my father laughing. He didn't do it enough, at least for my satisfaction. So when he did laugh, I cherished the memory, in fact, lately I've even captured a few on video tape—thus making them more than mere memories.

I've played one tape over several times recently, for two reasons: first, because he shared a story with me which I'm about to share with you, and second, because at the end of the story he laughed—a spontaneous, rumbling chuckle that is infectious. Everyone who has seen the tape has joined in the laughter.

A long time ago, as the story goes, Dad had a patient, quite a few miles from Walton, who was seriously ill with pneumonia. Since antibiotics had not yet hit the market, little could be done for this woman. She wasn't even in the hospital; Dad made trips to her house to do what he could, at least to make her as comfortable as possible and to support her family. Only time would tell if she was strong enough to survive this ancient killer.

It was the mid-thirties, so Dad was just starting out in his medical practice. Perhaps because of this, the family wanted to get a "second opinion" on Dad's diagnosis and treatment, from an older and more experienced doctor, one who had been treating pneumonia for many years. They found such a man in the southern part of Delaware County and asked Doc Eells if he would allow this second physician to examine the patient. Dad said that he had no objections, though he was a little nervous because this latecomer had a good reputation in Delaware County for curing cases of pneumonia. Was there something Dad had missed?

The older doctor arrived, carefully checked the patient and concurred: pneumonia it was and nothing more could be done in terms of specific treatment. Dad was quietly relieved and the family no doubt further comforted.

Unfortunately, the woman died a few days later. For Dad, this was sad, but not unexpected. According to him, a mortality rate of 20 to 30 percent was normal during those years. Life goes on, especially for a young doctor whose practice was becoming busier each month, so it seemed. Soon, her death was but a faint memory for him.

Sometime later Dad was participating in a local medical convention. During a break in the schedule, a man approached him and talked for a few moments in a friendly manner. It took Dad a little while to recall who he was and to connect this "legendary" gentleman with the earlier consultation. Actually, at this point, nothing had been said about their mutual patient. However, just as the man turned to depart, he stepped back toward Dad and began a new conversation.

"It's too bad about that patient down Hancock way, right Walter?" he queried.

"Yes, she died shortly after your visit, as I recall," answered Dad.

"Well, that's sad," came the response. "But what can you do when the heart stops beating?"

Heart stops beating?

It wasn't till later in the day that it dawned on Dad what this statement meant. Then he started laughing, because he knew why the "expert" had developed his reputation. People didn't die of pneumonia under his care, they died when their hearts stopped beating! That's what he had been putting on the death certificates; that's why he lost so few patients to the dreaded killer.

"It's hard to argue with that," Dad laughed into the tape. "When your heart stops beating, you die. No doubt about it."

If you watched the tape, you'd hear more than one person laughing.

A THIRD HAND

My mother, as previously noted, was a true partner to my father during his 63 years in medicine. This is not to suggest, however, that she was the only loyal lady in his office: over the years he was devotedly served by numerous women, almost all of whom functioned in the dual capacity of "secretary-nurse." One stands out in my mind, namely, Alienne Tweedie, distant cousin to my mother, hard-worker, and loyal supporter extraordinaire. "Tweedie," as we called her, worked with my father for about twenty-five years and became a part of our family. (She's still playing Scrabble with my parents.) One particular service brings a smile to my face to this day.

Doc Eells, as one could probably guess, was a softie as far as billing patients was concerned. He billed them and expected to be paid, just as he promptly paid his own bills. And most patients did. A "few" didn't, however. Dad never mentioned anything to the delinquents, but one person in particular found this inaction hard to swallow.

I remember that one day I was passing the office door in the evening when all patients were gone and it was finally quiet on that side of the Eells house. Except...I heard some mumbling coming from the other side of the main door, an angry sputtering from a familiar female voice. I peaked around the door and confronted the source: Miss Tweedie.

"Anything wrong?" I asked. She bit her tongue, perhaps a little surprised that she had been overheard. But I was by then in my late teens and ever-confident, so I persisted. Again, I asked the same question.

After a moment she answered: "It's your father. People owe him money, more people that you might expect. And some of them can pay. I know they can. I keep sending bills, with no response. But he won't call them or threaten to send them to a collector." "Oh," was about all I could say, somewhat knocked off guard. An awkward pause.

Tweedie looked at me for a moment and then opened up a desk drawer. "See the big file of cards?" she asked. "That's the good news. They've paid up. But look at this row," she said, pointing with obvious disgust. "These are the problem ones. Look how many there are. Some have been billed for months. Months!"

"What can we do?" I inquired, rather weakly.

"Not much," she answered with resignation. "Your Dad doesn't want me to do anything. But I let them know in one way or another," she sternly said, "that I'm not pleased. Especially those that can pay."

I'll bet you do, Tweedie, I thought. And I had no doubt that with some delinquents it produced results.

MISCHIEF

I don't know what came over me. I don't know why I was seized by this irresistible desire to do something out-of-the-ordinary, something weird or outrageous. But the "call" came and I answered it.

I was maybe fourteen or fifteen at the time. So far in life, I had shown few signs of abnormality. I was, in fact, quite conventional, a nice kid: respectful, responsible, a good student, pretty fair athlete—the whole bit. (Maybe this is why I did it?)

Anyway, I was alone one night in our third-floor attic, first listening to a Celtics play-off game, then speed reading one of Dad's historical novels. (Was it one of the more risky characters that set me off?) Then for a few moments I stared out the open window. It was open because it had been a warm spring day and remained pleasant into the night.

There was a break in the never-ending traffic up Townsend Street past our house, going toward the big city—Oneonta. It was quiet, "too quiet" as the movie saying goes. Unnervingly quiet. Not a sound. No voices from our house. Was the office empty so soon? Was anyone around? Was anyone alive?

Well, I wanted to have answers to these questions, I guess, because I couldn't take it anymore. Without making a sound, I turned off the light, carefully inched up the window, placed my nose against the screen, and screamed. I mean I belted out the loudest, most frightening, blood-curdling scream I could muster. It was a beaut. Then I ducked down so that no wandering eye could spot me and waited for a reaction, any response.

It wasn't long in coming: windows raised, doors opened, people spilled out into lawns on both sides of the street. "What was that?" people asked, huddled together, glancing suspiciously up and down the street. The milling around lasted for several minutes. By now, of course, I was laughing pretty hard, my back to the wall, hands covering my mouth. Gave them something to think about, didn't I? I felt rather superior. Until...

"Did you hear that scream?" Dad asked the family the next morning at breakfast.

I kept my eyes fixed on my cereal bowl. Everyone said they had heard something, except me. I remained silent. Finally, I answered: "I think I heard something, but I'm not sure what it was," came the "white lie."

"Well, I assume that it wasn't serious, that it was a practical joke," Dad said with an unusual degree of emotion in his voice. "And I didn't think it was funny. Several patients at the hospital were quite disturbed and hardly slept all night. I don't appreciate that kind of humor."

My gaze returned to the bowl. My screaming days were over.

FEET OF CLAY

Perfection? No, Dad wasn't and isn't perfect. Though, of course, I'm mainly trumpeting his positive features, perhaps a few examples of his fallibility should be noted.

First, I need to mention a trait that hits close to home, that is, one that I and other Eells males share in common. There's a gene missing somewhere in our bodies relating to mealtime activity. For Dad, this missing gene was glaringly apparent almost every night around six o'clock. By this time, Mom had already slaved over the hot stove for perhaps an hour, overcoming numerous interruptions from her demanding children.

"Dinner's ready," she would finally yell into the office. "Come to the table."

Dad usually made it to the table rather quickly, which was part of the problem: he did everything quickly. Maybe he should have walked backwards or in slow motion, because he would invariably arrive, sit down, pause for about three seconds, and sneak a bite or two. (Got to get back to the office, you know.) Sometimes Mom would see the "sneak attack" and say a few pertinent words through clenched teeth. At other times she missed it. But it probably wouldn't have mattered much. In fact, it didn't. Dad seemed to be constitutionally unable to sit and wait for the arrival of all the children and for Mom to place the last morsel of food before him. So, the inevitable would occur:

"Walter," she would say in exasperation, "couldn't you at least wait until I am seated?" Maybe an ever-so-slight exaggeration.

Is it comforting for the women-who-marry-Eellses to know that for the males it seems to be a universal trait? Not a good question.

Second, Dad had another genetic default, one apparently universal, not to Eellses, but to doctors—poor handwriting. I mean poor handwriting. Chicken scratches, if that is not too "fowl" a description.

I remember once when I was home from college when Dad asked me to help out with some clerical work. I was happy to volunteer, until I discovered what he had in mind.

"Can you type up some of my notes for the insurance records?" he asked innocently. I had been hoping that "clerical" meant filing or something. Wrong. I knew that I was in trouble even before glancing at the pages. Hoping against hope, I set up the experiment, placing the portable typewriter in just the right position, flexing my fingers, clearing my throat—anything to avoid looking at the handwritten pages in the folder. Eventually, though, I had to be a man. I opened the folder! My worst fears were immediately confirmed: an encyclopedia of gibberish. Glancing at the first paragraph, I was lucky to decipher one out of every five words. I started to get a headache. Feelings of guilt and anger washed over me. Now what was I to do? Help!

No one, however, came to my rescue. After a few frustrating minutes, I had to approach the "chicken" at the desk and confess my inadequacy.

"What do you mean they're hard to read?" he said, again innocently. "They're perfectly legible to me." Sure they are Dad, I said to myself as I headed for the aspirin in the medicine cabinet.

Finally, a word about psychology. Emotions play an important part in medicine, in the interaction of doctor and patient, especially when it concerns pain. Yet, at times Dad seemed a little bit too reserved, too removed from the psychological and physical reality of pain in his patients.

For example, I was once helping him suture a deep cut in a little girl's arm. The job was medically first rate, as usual. But the girl was frightened and the procedure no doubt also hurt her physically. Dad, however, wasn't very sensitive, very empathetic. Every time she groaned and flinched he snapped at me to keep her arm steady and dismissed her complaints rather casually. "You don't feel a thing," he said. "I numbed the whole area for you." Well, she sure looked like a girl in pain to me.

63

Later I asked Dad about his rather brusque treatment of this young patient. He just shrugged, as if to imply that he never felt much of the pain involved with his healing efforts.

"Dad," I said. "You know how painful some procedures can be, like a severe headache."

Then came the grabber: "Bob," he responded, "I can't remember ever having a headache."

Never had a headache! No wonder empathy sometimes seemed in short supply.

THE BEST TEACHER

The mother was worried: her son's temperature was high and Tylenol hadn't cut it down much; he had mysterious aches and pains; and he was thirsty, very thirsty. It was time—probably past time—to see a doctor.

At the doctor's it was a busy day. No time in his tight schedule to see this young patient. But someone on the staff was assigned to examine the boy. Maybe, still, a visit to the hospital emergency room could be avoided. The examination was brief, and her fears were relieved somewhat. Nothing was seriously wrong—probably the flu. Keep pumping him with fluids and get plenty of rest (sound familiar?).

Mom's relief was temporary, however, for her son didn't improve. In fact, his condition worsened. What to do?

Doc Eells? She hadn't seen him in several years. The old doctor was in his mid-eighties and kind of semi-retired. But maybe she should stop by his office and hope that he had an opening. Doc was always pretty good at sizing up situations.

There it is, 35 Townsend Street. "Chien Merchant." A familiar sign on the column. Wonder what it means?

She found several patients in the waiting room, a little discouraging. Is this semi-retirement? She didn't have to wait very long, though, perhaps thirty minutes.

"What are his symptoms?" asked the familiar face.

High fever, thirst, aches and pains. The face chewed on a toothpick. "Does the family have any history of diabetes?" asked the toothpick.

"Actually, yes," came the answer. "His grandmother. Now that you mention it, I think she died of complications resulting from diabetes. But at the other office they said it was the flu."

"Could be flu," answered the doctor, "but with those symptoms and family history, I would first suspect diabetes. Let's take blood and urine samples and see what we get."

Well, by the next day they had the answer: the blood sugar level had gone through the ceiling. Diabetes was the primary diagnosis. Intervention was immediately ordered so that the crisis could be confronted and the son's blood chemistry returned to normal. And none too soon!

Mom was now finally at ease. But, as she reflected, the "flu" explanation troubled her greatly.

Goes to show you, I guess, that in medicine experience is, <u>indeed</u>, frequently the best teacher.

PAIN

I was sitting in my kitchen waiting for the late show to begin. It was the summer of 1966. My friend and neighbor, Paul Eaton, was coming over to watch with me. I was feeling kind of depressed; maybe talking to Paul would cheer me up.

When Paul arrived I explained to him why I felt so blue: earlier in the day I had informed my parents that I was dropping out of my summer school calculus class, itself not such a bad move. It was, however, a crucial decision because it meant that I had decided, finally, that medicine was not in my future. Paul knew that I was trying calculus for a second time, with the hope of taking physics in the fall and then applying for medical school. So, applying was no longer an option.

Paul knew the context of my recent shift from history to medicine. He knew that my father had, with difficulty, asked me to try to complete the necessary courses to qualify for admission to medical school. It had been very hard for Dad to ask me. Dad realized that I loved history, but he also recognized that I was his best hope for continuing his tradition in medicine.

"You'll have a practice pretty much ready for you," Dad had said with some awkwardness. "Not many young men would be in such a position." True, I thought, so very true.

Funny thing is that I didn't resent the pressure from Dad. I liked biology in college, and I already had lots of practical experience in medicine, more no doubt than many medical students. So, I was willing to try, for him and for myself. But the calculus-physics stumbling block proved just too much to overcome.

"How did your parents take it?" asked Paul as we headed toward the living room TV.

"O.K. I guess," I responded. "Dad didn't look too happy, but he didn't say much right then."

"Did he bring it up later?" he inquired as we paused in the dining room.

"Yes, kind of," I replied. "Later he pulled me aside and suggested that maybe I could get some help with calculus, tutoring or something. I wasn't too pleased with that suggestion," I sighed. "He didn't seem willing to give up, even though I thought that I had made it clear to him."

I was beginning to speak more forcefully about the situation as we passed from the dining room into the living room. My voice had risen somewhat. I stopped and turned back to Paul. "Why does he have to be so stubborn about it?" I asked rhetorically. "Why can't he see that it isn't going to happen. I'm not going to become a doctor!"

Even before I finished the last sentence I knew that something was wrong. Paul had just touched my shoulder after glancing behind me toward the corner of the living room. My heart sank, for I realized instantly what was wrong. I slowly turned and took in the scene: sitting not ten feet away was my father. He had heard my last words. I hadn't been "whispering." Why, I thought in panic, hadn't I realized that Dad would be around somewhere? He never went to bed before midnight. I wanted to die.

Dad just stared at me, only for a few seconds, but it seemed like an eternity. He looked so sad and lonely, as if he was staring down a long road named "future," and some of the signposts he had expected to see had vanished, never to be seen again. Ever.

He slowly rose and walked across the length of the room, not even glancing at me. He climbed the stairs to his bedroom. At the top of the stairs he slammed the door. That was a first. My heart sank again. Dying would be a relief, I thought.

I didn't really watch the late show. I just sat there thinking of the pain I caused my father and the ache in my own heart. Dad and I never discussed the subject again. Over the years, of course, Dad has come to accept and take pride in my role as a history teacher. So, for him, it's probably ancient history. Now, for me too, it can be put to rest.

Shalom.

ADDENDUM

RECOLLECTIONS OF A COUNTRY DOCTOR
By a "Country Preacher"
(Joseph A. Hill)

When I moved to Walton, N.Y. in October, 1952, to begin my ministry, I was taken aside by one of the aging matriarchs of the congregation and told—quite confidentially, of course—that Walter E. Eells, M.D., a plump and graying middle-aged physician, also a parishioner and already a legend in the community, would be hard to get to know. He was rather standoffish and altogether too quiet; you never knew what he was thinking. Well, as the manse was not fully refurbished, our family was offered the use of the Eells's "cabin" which, as everybody around Walton knows, is situated on a rocky hillside along East Brook, about five miles out of town. That offer was good until we were able to move into our own quarters at 115 Townsend Street. During our sojourn at the cabin our families enjoyed several evenings together, eating supper and getting acquainted. The kids, as I remember, played games outside. Robert Hill and Ken Eells were only about six at the time, and they soon became fast friends. As for Walter and me, well, we hit it off from the start, and to this day I have never figured out why anyone would use words like standoffish to describe this legendary country doctor, except that one might misinterpret as aloofness the gentle reserve of one who enjoys listening more than impressing others with his wit. Anyway, looking back over four decades, I would venture to say that our friendship has stood up rather well, despite early predictions of a flawed relationship and the distance that has separated us since the mid-fifties.

* * * * *

Walter Eells has never been one to care about cars. I have no doubt that he could afford a Mercedes or two if he were charmed by such a status symbol. On the other hand, he probably couldn't tell a Mercedes from a Ford—and couldn't care less. I remember the old maroon Plymouth that stood in the driveway at 35 Townsend Street when I first knew Doc Eells, as he was known around Walton. Well, when the old Plymouth was beginning to falter on the way over to the Post Office, Doc called the Dodge dealer (I seem to recall the name Williams Motors) and said, "Ya got somethin' down there to send up?" Most folks go and look around a showroom, or shop around for the best deal, find out how much their trade-in is worth, and pick out the color of their new chariot. Not Walter. Too much bother! "Send somethin' up." Williams Motors, post-haste, brought up a shiny new bronze colored '53 Dodge sedan, which served the Eells family several years thereafter. I had never known anyone before who thought of an automobile as just a way to get about. If I had any doubts about this, they disappeared when I asked Walter, "How many cylinders?" and he replied, "Oh, I don't know."

* * * * *

Walter Eells seldom drove the family car, for as I have said, he didn't care much about cars; driving them was "a bother." I always suspected that there was another reason: he was short of stature—probably couldn't see over the steering wheel very well. Maybe, too, he liked to have company on his house calls in the country...out in Ox Bow Hollow or up McGibbon Hollow or somewhere down around Rock Rift (which has long since been submerged beneath the Pepacton Reservoir). Now and then—quite often, in fact—my sermon preparation was interrupted by a phone call. It was Walter. "Doin' anything special?" "Nothing I can't put aside. What's up?" "Thought you might like a ride in the country. I have to see old Mabel, up Pines Brook." "Sure, I'll be glad to go along," I'd say. A few minutes later, the bronze '53 Dodge sedan (it was a V-8, by the way—I looked under the hood) swung into the driveway at the manse—the Covenanters tend to say parsonage—and Walter slid over to the passenger side while I got behind the wheel. Doctors nowadays, by and large, don't make house calls; but Doc Eells was of the old school. If someone was sick enough to need a doctor, chances are they were too sick to go to the doctor's office, so the doctor went to the house with his well worn black bag.

On the way up Pines Brook, or down Beerston way, I got a complete run-down of Mabel's family tree, all the kinfolk back several generations. I heard about the Fitches and the Doigs and the St. Johns. Names like Rufus and Cyrus and Fannie and Sadie were common in the early days, and Walter knew many of these old-timers, if not personally, at least by hearsay.

Some of the sick folk were Methodists, some Baptists, and a few were Congregationalists—even a Catholic or two. I dare say some of the folks had no church connections at all, and maybe the Doc was thinking that these latter patients needed to meet a preacher...and even start going to church. These trips to the country with the Walton doctor taught me lessons I hadn't learned in seminary. I have no doubt that my own capacity for empathy and caring began to develop as I observed the bedside manner of this country doctor who went the second mile with his medicines— not the least of which was his gentle and personable way at the bedside of his patients.

* * * * *

In the early fifties, when we moved to Walton, the Delaware Valley Hospital had been in operation for only a year, and up to that time Smith Hospital, which was Dr. Eells's own medical center, had been the only such facility for miles around. Dr. Eells continued to do surgery "across the street," as he always said—that was where Smith Hospital was located. In those days not everything was so tightly controlled by Albany as it is now, especially in the medical practice. Today I would probably not be allowed in the OR, unless I were the patient. On a number of occasions, back then in 1953 or '54, the Doc asked if I would give him and his surgical staff a hand. "What's up, Doc?" I wondered,

71

and he said they were having to "pin a hip," which meant repairing an elderly woman's broken hip. It fell to my lot to stand or sit (I forget which) at the foot of the bed and, taking hold of the patient's foot, apply just the right amount of traction on the leg, so that surgical screws and metal plates could be attached.

Once I was present to observe a C Section—no pulling this time—and I was amazed at the "miracle" of fetal development and the wonder of God's creative work in the womb.

There were important lessons in health care. A young minister needs to learn about practical matters like this; Walter Eells knew this, and I was the better for having had operating room "experience" which is the privilege of not many clergy persons. The health of the soul is the pastor's principal concern; but isn't the bodily health of his flock a matter for pastoral attention as well? Many times, remembering my Walton days—Smith Hospital, the Doctor's office at 35 Townsend Street, and the house calls in the country—I've been prompted to say to my sick friends what the elder John said to his friend Gaius (III John, vs. 2): "I pray that all may go well with you and that you may be in good health, just as it is well with your soul."

Morning, afternoon, and evening they came with their complaints, and he listened—and dozed—while they described their aches and pains. Weary after six days of this listening, diagnosing, and prescribing, he showed up in church on Sunday morning—Covenanters tend to say Sabbath morning—finally enjoying his day of rest. I knew that he had earned his day of rest, so, if he appeared to be dozing during the sermon, who was I to pass judgement? It's okay to shut one's eyes during a prayer, but during the sermon? Well, "Mrs. E" was mortified to have a dozing husband sitting next to her while I was droning on about sin or something equally orthodox. Once I heard her say, "Walter, can't you stay awake for just an hour?" That was probably the only time she ever asked that question, for his reply—"I wasn't asleep"—was followed by a point by point review of the sermon, including the text itself. I've often wondered: when I speak, people listen, but do they **hear**?

* * * * *

Dr. Eells knew where he could get a good cup of coffee, late at night. After the waiting room was emptied out and necessary paperwork done, Dr. Eells would make rounds "across the street"—meaning Smith Hospital—swing by the Post Office to drop off forms and other kinds of red tape ("It's getting worse all the time," he used to say), then coast into our driveway at 115 Townsend Street. The coffee pot was usually on, and we always enjoyed the late night snack we shared with him, and the coffee, which was inevitably too strong for him. "That's rugged," he would say. "And how about this cheese, is it rugged too?" I would ask. "Pretty **strong** stuff! Rat cheese," he would say. I can't remember any profound topics that we discussed, but looking back I can see that even the commonplace, when shared by friends, becomes special and extraordinary.

* * * * *

It was typical of Walter Eells to let me in on happenings around the village. One chilly night in, I'd say, 1955, Walter had been "across the river"—his euphemism for making rounds at Delaware Valley Hospital. From over there somewhere, he called on the telephone and said, rather excitedly for him, "Camp's Feed Mill is on fire, and boy, it's goin' up. Why dontcha come down." I seem to recall that, as it was quite late at night, he was the one who first saw the small beginnings of what became a spectacular blaze that lit up the night sky and warmed the hundreds of onlookers as fire fighters worked into the wee hours of the morning in a futile attempt to save at least part of the old mill. He and I stood by, like so many others, mesmerized by the towering inferno, the likes of which neither of us had ever seen before. "Isn't it scary," I remarked to him, "to realize that a business can thrive for generations and go up in smoke in one night?" And Walter replied, "Yep."

* * * * *

Back in the fifties, Mr. Bates and his sister, Vida Bates, were still peddling homemade butter to folks in the village. I would see them going up Townsend Street in a horse-drawn buggy. In the winter, when the village streets were snow-covered, they rode in a sleigh. This was a curiosity to Barbara and me, and especially to our very young children, Robert, Linda, and Tim (we called him Timmy then). To Walter Eells this special delivery was hardly a curiosity, for having grown up in Walton, he had seen the two Bateses going up and down Townsend Street in their sleigh over many years. The real curiosity for him was the procession of dogs that walked behind the Bateses' sleigh to make a meal of the "road apples" which the horses left on the snow-covered street. "A nice, steaming meal" is how Walter described them. "The dogs just love 'em," he said..."Heh, heh, heh." A Yankee sense of humor, to be sure.

AS I RECALL

Mostly, my stories come from my own experiences or from interviews with my father. It has been difficult to get him to sit down and compose stories himself. Occasionally, however, this has happened. I include the following recollection authored by him to give you an idea of the "gold mine" that could have been tapped all along.

This little boy perhaps four years old was brought to my office on November 14, 1941. I sent him across the street to Smith Hospital where he remained until December 31, 1941. He was the son of Emil Baldauf of Delancey, New York. Mr. Baldauf had been converted to Mormonism in Germany and then came to this country and bought a farm near Delancey, New York.

The father told me that John came out to the barnyard and asked him to set him on the horse. The child fell off the horse and hit the ground. The horse became nervous and stomped on the child's left arm causing an open fracture of the humerus.

I put him in traction. One day the nurse reported that when she was bathing John she heard a crackling sound on his chest. I checked my books and decided he had gas gangrene infection and started him on sulfanilamide. In a few days someone reported the child was very cyanic and I recalculated the dose and found he was getting twice what I had ordered.

His wound healed and he went home on December 31, 1941, as I stated above.

On March 28, 1942, he came back with osteomyelitis in the humerus. I removed about half of the humerus and he was in the hospital three or four days. He went home April 1, 1942. He returned later, I don't have the date, and I removed the other half of the humerus. I have not seen him since then. I understand he and his sister run the dairy farm. As far as I know he has never had any other sickness.

Part III

Essays in Memory of Walter E. Eells, M.D.

COUNTRY DOCTOR

Third Edition
2001

Robert J. Eells

ROOM AT THE INN

December 1944. The world was at war. The German army had launched a major counter-offensive in an effort to push the Allies back into the sea. It was not to be. They were stalled for two basic reasons: they ran short of gasoline and they confronted the "elements"—a brutal winter which buried them and everyone in mountains of snow and numbed them with bone-chilling temperatures. Many men died on both sides and the real heroes proved to be the medics, who risked their own lives to tend to the wounded.

Thousands of miles away in the peaceful village of Walton, New York, another crisis occurred which also called upon the administrative and medical skills of a small-town doctor and his wife. They rose to the occasion, just like those far-away medics.

Dr. Walter Eells and his wife, Katherine, faced their own "battle" when a fire broke out at Smith Hospital on December 10, 1944. The small hospital (a wood structure) was filled with patients (thirty was full for Smith), and not only was there snow on the ground that day, but the temperature had plunged to $-12°F!$, a possible calamity when attempting to transport patients.

All the patients were evacuated safely. Several ambulances responded to the emergency as well as friends and neighbors, eager to hurry people to their destinations. The big question of the day, however, was where to take them? Quickly, Doctor Eells made three decisions: some—the least ill—were sent home; some of the most serious were sent to other area hospitals; but a major obstacle remained: a few of the seriously ill didn't want to be sent away. They pleaded with the doctor not to send them to other hospitals.

"What are we going to do, Katherine?" the doctor asked.

It didn't take her long to come up with an answer: "We'll have to put them in our house. We can free up three bedrooms if we put the baby (me at nine months!) in our room and keep

Eleanor (three years old) in her small room off the master bedroom. That will give us enough space for the remaining patients (six in all)."

"That's a big burden," responded her husband. "You'll have to take care of two small children and cook and help care for several other people. Are you sure you want to do this?"

"I don't see any other way," she answered quietly. "They really want to be under your care here in Walton. As long as we have a nurse on at all times, we can manage."

Well, they did manage, though they had no idea at the outset that this arrangement would last for ten weeks! During that whole time, they cared for no fewer than five patients at a time, so it was usually two per room. Three daily meals were provided by the good wife, round-the-clock nurses tended to the regular medical needs of the patients (with assistance from Mrs. E.), and Doc Eells just had to jump upstairs to make his "rounds." The doctor's appointment book was full during these weeks, meaning that he saw between thirty and forty people per day in his first-floor office in the same house at 35 Townsend Street. It was a hectic pace for all. By the way, Dr. Eells also performed one appendectomy and delivered two babies up on the second floor!

It's hard to imagine anything like that happening today. Quite understandable. At the same time, hasn't something valuable been lost? Perhaps forever?

The most amazing thing to me is how my mother could be so selfless, so willing to allow her own home to serve as a hospital. For most moms just raising two youngsters would have been more than enough responsibility. Mom, you were truly remarkable! As always.

NEITHER SNOW NOR SLEET

The young doctor got the call in the afternoon. It was in the middle of winter, 1930. He had been practicing medicine for only a few months, mostly cooperating with and learning from his step-father, Dr. William Smith. The call came from an anxious father-to-be who lived in Trout Creek, several miles down Route 206 from Walton.

"Dr. Eells, we need your help," implored the man. "My wife is having a baby; she's in labor right now, I think, and I can't locate Dr. Smith. He's our regular Doc. We know you're working with him. Can you come? I don't know what more I can do."

"If I can't find Dr. Smith, I'll come myself," came the reply.

Well, Dr. Eells couldn't find his step-father, but keeping his promise wasn't going to be easy. There was a lot of snow on the ground, and it was magnified by many hours of drifting from the howling wind. The wind had died down, but getting to Trout Creek wouldn't be easy.

He contacted the police and received the worst possible news: Route 206 was officially closed. He suggested putting chains on his car, but they discouraged him. Even chains wouldn't help much. How, he wondered, could he get through?

Horse and buggy? Why not try? (This was seventy years ago and some people still had available this "alternative" means of travel.) He called around, found a two-horse team and sleigh, hitched it up, then had to decide what route to take. 206 was still risky because of the numerous hills, so he decided to attempt the round-about way, toward Rock Royal, then traveling back roads, down into Trout Creek from the other direction.

It took quite some time, but the doctor finally arrived—to the great relief of the anxious caller. The husband was right: the woman was, indeed, in labor. The young doctor tried to act confident, nonetheless.

81

Though the woman's signs seemed normal in most respects, still two problems remained: they were alone—success would depend only on the assistance of the doctor and husband; and the house had no electricity—so as darkness approached, maintaining adequate light would prove problematic.

As darkness descended, the doctor gave the husband his most important assignment—tending the lantern. "Keep it close, with a steady hand," came the order. "I'll try," came the shaky response.

As her labor reached its final stages, the woman became more and more stressed, so Doc Eells administered a sedative (ether perhaps?). So, in the final moments before birth this was the scene: the husband nervously holding the lantern, trying to look and not look at the same time; the woman trying to push, cooperate, and relax; and the inexperienced doctor—administering a sedative with his left hand and delivering a baby with his right hand. (Almost seems like a Norman Rockwell portrait, from behind the husband, of course.)

The results of the early morning delivery included a relieved doctor, a happy mother, an exhausted father, and a healthy baby girl. Incidentally and ironically, the girl lived almost a normal life span, but died a couple of years before the attending physician. He lived to be 97!

DR. STRANGELOVE

My sister-in-law, Sharon Caffery, taped a conversation with Ron Gray, Dad's son-in-law, at the visitation hours the night before the funeral. Ron had an amusing event to record.

As a background, I'll remind readers about Dad's reluctance to drive. Mom did most of the driving, but when she was unavailable, the good doctor would call on anyone handy to drive him all over kingdom come, or at least Delaware County. I did it, as did his nephew, Walt Eells, and the Rev. Joe Hill. Ron, too, was occasionally called into duty when he and my sister, Eleanor, were visiting Walton.

According to Ron, Dad received a phone call at about 2:30 a.m. from a worried husband who reported that his wife was in great pain, so much so he feared to move her. Could the doctor come out to the house?

Sure, why not. Dad rolled out of bed and walked across the hallway to Ron's room and knocked on the door.

"Ron, can you help me out? I've got to visit a patient out in the country."

"Sure, no problem," answered the sleepy son-in-law. Ron proceeded to drive Dad over 30 miles, all the way to the back side of Bear Mountain. Finding the house, however, was only half the problem: Ron also had to get Doc Eells up a rather steep hill, because the car couldn't navigate the long, winding entrance. So, Dad carried the bag and Ron carried Dad—on his back—up the incline in the dark.

Arriving at the house, Dad went to work. Apparently, the woman was experiencing menopause and had convinced herself that the pain was unbearable. Doc Eells did his best to calm her down and assure her that her condition was not serious, not life threatening. He gave her a mild sedative and some pain medication. "The woman was just a little wacky, that's most of it," Dad said with a smile.

Strange, too, was the story the husband related to Ron while the two hovered in the background. According to the husband, flying saucers had been visiting his mountain retreat for some time. The husband had been observing them carefully and had even gathered up an occasional sample of debris from a passing flight. Further, one such piece had been transported proudly by him to Syracuse University for scientific examination.

Well, Ron listened with fascination for quite awhile. He later shared the full details with his father-in-law as the two carefully walked back to the car. By consensus they agreed that both husband and wife were a little "wacky." They had a good laugh all the way back to the house, which continued through breakfast.

By the way, Dad received $5.00 in payment for his trouble that night.

THE FRONTIERSMAN

In midlife Dad had few hobbies, except reading historical novels, watching me and my cousin, Bruce Henderson, play high school basketball, and, of course, obsessing over Scrabble. Earlier, however, he spent some time hunting—woodchucks to be precise. For a few years he tramped all over the back woods surrounding Walton, helping the dairy farmers rid themselves of those troublesome little creatures—whose front doors could break a horse's leg or tip over a tractor. Well, over time he became a pretty good shot and dispatched more than a few of them to woodchuck heaven.

Usually he hunted alone. Mom thought that he could spend his valuable free time more profitably. She even began to doubt his reported "kills," since he came home empty handed. If he wanted exercise, why not just walk around town with her every day or so?

Everything changed rather dramatically one day when a couple of McNaney relatives came down from Utica for a visit— a nephew, Thomas (Tuck), and a niece, Carolyn. After conferring briefly with them, Dad walked into the kitchen and announced: "Katherine, I'm going hunting and the kids have volunteered to chauffeur me around and keep me company."

With little enthusiasm she replied, "Are you sure they want to go along?"

"They do, and they'll have a good time."

All three piled into the car and headed for the back roads, woodchuck country. Tuck drove, Carolyn sat in the back seat as a spotter, and Uncle Doc rode "shotgun" or "rifle gun" in this case, since his weapon was a 22-gauge rifle.

They drove around for awhile, saw a few targets, and Uncle Doc took a couple of errant shots. No luck. They eventually turned around and headed back home and were close to town when Carolyn blurted out, "Uncle, I see one off to the right, past the big oak tree, about fifty yards away."

"I see him," whispered her uncle.

Tuck eased the car to a stop and hunter and helpers quietly exited. They climbed over a stone fence and crept up behind a nearby fallen log. The hunter steadied his rifle against the log, breathed in and out slowly, and squeezed off a round. Bulls eye!

"I think I hit him," Uncle Doc yelled. "Go check it out for me."

They did, and he had. On their way back to the car, though, they were stopped in their tracks when they heard their uncle shout: "Wait, I have an idea. One of you pick him up and bring him back to the car."

"What do you mean, pick him up?" Carolyn replied nervously.

"Just hold him by his tail; he won't bite you," came the confident response.

Tuck looked at Carolyn. Carolyn looked at Tuck. Just as Carolyn was about to speak, Tuck raised his arms and announced: "Hey, I'm sorry, but I'm driving, remember?"

So the dutiful niece carried the prize back to the car, dropped it at her uncle's feet, hoping her unpleasantness had ended. Not quite.

Her uncle ushered her into the back seat, lowered the window as far as it would go, picked up the dead woodchuck and gave her another command: "Carolyn, stick out your hand and hold him by his tail again. We're going to take him back with us. Don't worry, it's not far. Your aunt doesn't believe I ever hit anything. This will prove her wrong!"

Carolyn did as she was told, carrying the woodchuck with her right hand and holding her nose with her left—all the way home. Upon arrival all three walked around to the back door where Uncle Doc called out: "Katherine, come here a minute. Carolyn has something to show you."

Aunt Katherine came out, gazed upon the outstretched hand, gasped, and quickly retreated to the safety of the kitchen. She never again doubted her husband's hunting stories. Really.

ANXIETY (1)

Many stories came my way during the visitation hours the day before my father's funeral. Here is one of them.

A former patient, Bob Seibert, then about twenty, was having trouble with his tonsils. They had been bothering him for several years. Finally, Doc Eells recommended having them removed.

The day arrived and Bob somehow made it to Smith Hospital, hoping for an "uneventful" day. A nurse on the second floor—the location of the operating room—showed him where to undress and what to wear. So, a few minutes later he was nervously pacing up and down the hallway outside the operating room, waiting his turn since the doctor was busy with an earlier operation.

Back and forth he wandered. It seemed like an eternity to him, so much so that he had just about decided to leave. "I don't really need this operation," he said to himself. "My throat doesn't feel that bad." He swallowed a few times just for confirmation.

Before the rebellion could be launched, though, he thought he heard someone call out his name. He paused and listened intently.

"Bob, Bob Seibert," came the voice from <u>inside</u> the operating room. "Come in here."

Bob inched his way toward the door. "Doc, did you ask me to come in?" he almost whispered.

"Yes, I need your help," replied the surgeon. "It's O.K. Come on in."

Help? What could Doc Eells mean? Here I am, he thought, standing in my own gown waiting for an operation on <u>me</u>, and he wants my help?

Gingerly he opened the door. He took a few tentative steps and stopped. Doc Eells was alone at the moment, though it soon became apparent that a nurse was coming in and out of the room.

The doctor was bending over the patient, a very small patient, with his back toward the guest. Now what?

The doctor turned and motioned Bob to come around to the other side of the operating table. Bob obeyed and as he circled around, he realized that the patient was an infant, at most a few days old.

Bob took a deep breath, not quite believing what was happening to him. But it was happening, because the command quickly came: "Take hold of this instrument at the end and just hold it still. I'll let you know when to move it and where."

Bob grabbed ahold and then proceeded to "assist" Dr. Eells in performing a circumcision on a new-born boy!

"A few minutes later, he took out my tonsils," Bob told me with great delight at the visitation. We laughed together and shared this story with others around us.

"There was no one like him," Bob concluded. "He was special!"

ANXIETY (2)

Apparently, pacing nervously in the hallway outside the operating room was a fairly common experience at Smith Hospital. Here's another example, this time a second-hand account, from Jackie Spear.

Some time ago Jackie experienced abdominal pains which Doc Eells quickly diagnosed as appendicitis. All the arrangements were made, and on the date selected Jackie showed up the night before to prepare for an early surgery the following day.

On the morning of the operation everything was progressing normally, at least for the surgeons. Dad and Dr. Harry Wilbur had become very proficient at removing this particular offending organ—so much so that I once heard Dad comment he could probably take out an appendix in his sleep.

Not everyone, naturally, was so relaxed or confident. Waiting outside was Jackie's husband, Wendell. For Wendell, or any husband, an appendectomy is rarely a "minor" surgery. Sitting or pacing, he no doubt tried to avoid thinking about all the worst scenarios.

Inside the operating room the doctors quickly located the correct appendage.

"Now this is interesting," Dad pointed out to Harry. "I think Wendell is just outside. Let's bring him in."

So the call went out, stopping the husband in mid-stride. "Wendell, come in here a minute. We've got something to show you."

Perhaps Wendell was confused for a moment. Enter the operating room? But, then again, this was Dr. Eells, and he ran his practice and hospital a little differently than most other doctors. That was part of the beauty of a small town and its "general practice" of medicine.

"Doc, do you really want me in there?" Wendell asked through the door.

"Sure," replied Doc Eells, "Just come in and stand off to the side of the table."

With some trepidation, he screwed up his courage and inched his way into the room. Following directions, he moved to the side (and foot) of the table, looking over Dad's shoulder.

"Just a minute," said the surgeon. "There, I've got it."

At that precise moment, in one fluid movement, Dr. Eells turned toward Wendell, extending his right arm. Perched at the end of a small instrument lay the appendix. Right there, not two feet from Wendell's face.

"Look at the size of this thing," noted the doctor with fascination. "I've rarely seen one so big. We're just in time. It could have ruptured at any moment."

Big or not, Wendell began to feel a little queasy. You see, it was not just the appendix, *per se*, that confronted him. Dad had yet to sever the appendix from the intestines, so when he thrust it out toward Wendell, it brought along several feet of internal organs!

Perhaps Wendell blurted out something like, "Looks good, Doc. Nice job." In any event, he quickly retreated from the room, seeking a breath of fresh air. He made it, but never forgot the experience.

I guess that there are all kinds of "surgeries." At least, there used to be.

A DATE TO REMEMBER

Dad was a family man. He loved being a father, and even though Mom did most of the "bringing up" at the Eells' house, Dad was always there for us, always close when we needed a helping hand. Perhaps it's true that at the end of his life his greatest emotional support came from his daughter, Eleanor, but I think that at the outset he wanted a son (or sons), hoping to get an M.D. out of at least one of them. This didn't happen, of course, but I can still imagine the joy in his heart the day he helped bring me into the world in 1944. I was born at home in an upstairs bedroom, a fairly common practice at the time and one which Janice and I continued with our two children, Rick and Anne.

My father kept his annual appointment books in the waiting room of his office and from time to time I have perused them, somewhat in amazement I must say. Even a glance will demonstrate how busy he was on a typical day. For most days, in most years, twenty to forty names would be listed, including notations about medicines dispensed and charges made (the total bill rarely exceeding five dollars until the second half of his practice). All of this took place usually in late morning through evening hours because early morning was set aside for rounds at Smith Hospital or for operations on his patients or assisting other doctors, like Harry Wilbur.

For a busy man, though, he kept pretty complete records. So, this past summer (2000) when my sister and I were sorting through all the "stuff" my parents collected during sixty years of marriage and medicine, I made my way into the waiting room to box up the appointment books.

At that moment it hit me! I suddenly realized that I had never checked out what happened on the day of my birth, March 14, 1944. "I wonder how he announced to the world that special event?" I asked myself. I quickly discovered the correct volume and page, and it looked familiar at first glance: there Dad had made all the typical notations about patients (thirty plus!), medicine, et al. Then I smiled. Then I laughed.

"Eleanor," I called out. "Come here a minute. I've got something to show you."

After a moment or two, she arrived and I handed her the book.

"Look, it's March 14, 1944. What do you think?"

"Looks pretty normal to me," she replied.

"Normal?" I shot back. "Normal? But there's no mention of me! Nothing! Nada! He brought me into the world right above our heads and never even mentioned it!"

Then we both laughed because it was so much like Dad. It would never have occurred to him to record what happened during a "break"—even if it also included some medical assistance. Upstairs was family business.

So, my ego really wasn't damaged. Much.

A DAY TO FORGET

I was home on a summer break, having spent my first year in Pennsylvania at Geneva College. I had been helping Dad with his medical duties—sometimes with light lab work, occasionally even assisting him in the operating room. On this particular day, though, I remember having other plans: I had arranged to go fishing with one of my high school buddies who was also home on vacation. It was not to be.

Late in the morning Dad found me finishing a snack and made a request: "Bob," he said innocently, "Harry and I are pinning a hip on an elderly woman this afternoon. We are short one nurse. Would you help us?"

"Sure, Dad," I managed to say between bites. "What time?"

"Around one-thirty," he answered on his way to the office.

It wasn't my first choice and sounded a little gruesome, but I could always go fishing another day.

I wasn't as prepared as I thought I would be, however. It was, indeed, gruesome. Opening up the flesh on top of the hip all the way to the bone caused a fair amount of bleeding. The surgeons stopped the bleeding, but then the real "fun" began. Dad had to drill into the bone, manually with a hand drill.

I grimaced watching it. I can still remember the awful sound it made. Not my favorite noise!

Most of my discomfort, though, came from my specific duties that day. I was assigned a place at the patient's feet where I was told to hold the proper foot at a particular angle. It didn't seem so bad at first. She was an old lady who couldn't have weighed more than one hundred pounds. But I also had to keep the foot elevated a little bit off the table. My lower back soon started to feel a little strain; still, though, I could manage because the weight was minimal.

The real trouble began after the hip was successfully pinned. First, they had to take an X-ray to check the position of the pin. It took the nurse a long time—or so it seemed to me—to bring back the developed film. When she arrived Dad said: "Give the film to Bob and let him put it up to the light." Simple enough I thought. But, alas, I blew it.

You see, I couldn't figure out how to position the film correctly in front of the light. I held it one way, then another, then a third—hoping to find the right angle. Each time I turned the film I was responding to a direct instruction from one of the doctors. What was obvious to them was beyond my grasp. Finally, they couldn't take it any more. Dr. Wilbur abruptly backed away from the table, ripped off his gloves, and threw them on the floor. He marched around the table, yanked the film from my hand, and with one swift move planted it in the correct position. To say that I felt humiliated would be an understatement.

Second, my troubles were not yet finished. They still had to put the leg in a body cast—all the way from the ankle up the leg to the waist. Guess who had the pleasure of holding the leg again, in the right position, slightly elevated? What took about twenty minutes felt like 200. I had never experienced lower back pain as bad. I shifted from leg to leg, arched my back, rolled my shoulders, anything to relieve the strain. Nothing worked. Sweat appeared on my forehead and began to head south. I tried to wipe it away with my shoulders with little success. Once or twice I heard someone say, "Keep it straight, Bob." I assumed in my fog that it came from one of the doctors.

Just about when I thought I would fall to the floor, taking leg and patient along with me, I heard these glorious words: "It's done, Bob, you can let go and relax." I had survived. Barely.

Walking back across the street to my house a few minutes later, I still felt pain in my lower back and in my ego.

I did get to go fishing later in the summer, though.

OUCH!

Long before sterilized, throw-away syringes, my father would boil the whole unit—glass and needle—in his trusty Bunsen burner. This cleansing proved more than adequate for his purposes. Yet, the continual use of the needles and their cleansing made them dull rather quickly. Dull needles don't penetrate the skin very easily. Not wanting to cause his patients undue pain, he would sharpen them when they reached the critical point of dullness—usually when patients began to complain.

Dad used a whetstone to sharpen the needles. With practice he got pretty good at it. In just a few minutes the needle was as good as new, well almost.

At any rate, one day during the war a certain patient made the following observation after a shot: "Doc, what are you using there, a fountain pen? That hurt!" Time for some more sharpening, thought the young doctor.

Later in the day he went to work on the needle, and after a few moments it looked good to the naked eye. One or two more strokes he guessed would do the trick.

But the unexpected happened: the whetstone slipped, and the sharpened needle nicked his finger, drawing blood. "Idiot," he said through clenched teeth to no one in particular.

No big deal. He stopped the bleeding, put a bandage on it, and gave it no more thought; until, that is, several months later when he received a call from another doctor in town.

"Walter," the physician began, "remember that physical you took for the army?" (Dad gave army physicals during the war and was also required to take one from time to time.)

"Yes, of course I do. Anything wrong?" Dad inquired suspiciously.

"Overall, you're in fine shape," continued the caller, "but one lab test came back positive."

"Oh, which one?" asked Dad.

"Well, the one for syphilis, Walter. I thought you should know right away so you can start treatment."

"Thanks, I will," Dad responded softly. "Would you be in charge, with the treatment, that is?"

"Gladly. Come over this afternoon, and we'll get started."

Dad hung up the phone and stared at the wall for a long time. Syphilis? Where in the world, he wondered, did syphilis come from?

Then he recalled the needle, the nick, and the patient. That very patient—seen several months before—had, in fact, been suffering from venereal disease. The doctor had infected himself!

Treatment began—with small doses of arsenic—and it was successful. Further tests were all negative.

This episode happened, however, in 1943, the year of my conception. Maybe that's why I'm left-handed, nearsighted, and have lost a "little" of my hair. Maybe...

THE EXTRA MILE

Perusing one of the many letters of congratulations on the milestone of my father's ninetieth birthday, this reflection jumped out at me.

A woman, I'll call her Lilly, recalled that she was one of my father's first deliveries, so it must have been about 1930 or 1931. Dad was, of course, single then and filled with the enthusiasm so typical of young physicians. But he had other special qualities, too, qualities which would stick with him throughout his sixty years in practice.

Lilly mentioned that her father died just a couple of years after her birth. Later in Lilly's life her mother recounted to her some of the events surrounding this tragedy, one of which involved Dr. Eells. It seems that Lilly, too, was sadly somewhat of a burden during these difficult days, because she was sick with the measles. In fact, she was quite seriously ill, so much so that she couldn't be left alone for more than a few minutes.

Her mother, thus, had to provide for her care and at the same time tend to all of the other painful duties relative to the funeral. What was to be done with Lilly during the funeral? Lilly obviously couldn't be taken along to the service and the following hours of grieving. Her mother's friends also wanted to show their support by attending the funeral. Perhaps one of them offered to stay with the ailing child—the letter doesn't say. What it does say, though, gripped my heart, making me reread it several times:

"My mother told me years later, Dr. Eells, how you came to the house and sat with me, staying much of the afternoon, so that my mother could attend my father's funeral. I've never forgotten that story."

Neither have I.

FOURTH COUSIN, ONCE REMOVED

About ten years ago my parents paid us a visit to our Oak Forest, Illinois, home. We were glad to host them, anticipating much conversation and frequent Scrabble games. It turned out, however, not to be a normal visit.

Dad was hardly in the front door before he asked me if I had ever heard of Richard Eells, the pre-Civil War doctor. To my chagrin, I denied any knowledge. He then proceeded to give me some of the details concerning this Dr. Eells, especially his part in the Underground Railroad in Illinois.

"He was from Quincy," Dad announced. "How far is Quincy from here?"

"It's on the Mississippi, so a few hours west by car," I replied.

"Why don't we ride over for a visit?" he suggested.

"It would require an overnight, meaning I would miss two class days," I responded.

I could tell by the look on his face that he was disappointed. Before I could relent, though, and offer to drive them anyway, he said, "Let's fly." Of course, we did, at a moment's notice. We flew to St. Louis from Chicago, then up the river to Quincy. We planned a round-trip on the same day.

Even before reaching Quincy, we had an adventure. At St. Louis we boarded a "puddle hopper" piloted by two men who in appearance resembled teenagers. There was no one on the plane except the three Eellses. Shortly before take off the co-pilot looked back and made a request:

"Say, folks, would you all move back about two rows. It's better for the plane's balance."

We exchanged glances and did as ordered. It worked: we arrived safely. It was, by the way, an absolutely gorgeous trip, flying in October, following the river, only a thousand feet or so above ground. The leaves were turning, and the vision was stunning.

We were met at the airport and given a tour of the Eells house by Quincy citizens who were attempting to raise money for the restoration of the old homestead—where slaves were hidden on their way north to Canada and freedom. The committee was delighted to see us and gave us all the history of the house, the last surviving one on the "railroad" in Illinois. They also described all the exciting events surrounding the arrest of Richard Eells for hiding a slave and the famous trial which followed. The judge at the trial was Stephen Douglas (of Lincoln-Douglas debates) and subsequent attorneys on appeal after his conviction were William Seward and Salmon Chase— both members of Lincoln's cabinet. After Richard Eells' death, the case made it all the way to the Supreme Court where, ironically, it was upheld on the eve of the Civil War.

Needless to say, Dad was making mental notes of everything. I could tell by his questions and comments that he was immensely proud of his distant cousin. He kept the discussion going on the return flight and even suggested I do further research on this subject and publish an article (maybe someday).

I predicted his behavior upon his return to Walton, and I was right. He sent a check to the trust in charge of the restoration and began writing a summary of the trip for the next Eells family bulletin. Dad was so wonderfully predictable!

HABIT

Late in life Dad had two obsessions: researching the Eells family history and playing Scrabble. During the day he concentrated on the former, at night the latter.

Almost every evening different individuals would show up at 35 Townsend Street to challenge the "master" at his favorite word game. Dad usually prevailed, to the astonishment of all concerned. He rarely forgot how to spell a word, especially words with letters like x, y, and z.

That this obsession was close to his heart was never more apparent than on December 31, 1997. On that day he was in intensive care at Delaware Valley Hospital in Walton, having suffered a fairly serious heart attack the previous day. I arrived on January 1, 1998, and he looked weak and thin. The nurse agreed with my assessment and remarked that on the thirty-first his appearance was even worse—in and out of consciousness, as he struggled against the pain.

"A remarkable man, though," she remarked. "You wouldn't believe what happened yesterday afternoon. [Actually, I thought, I probably would believe.]

"What happened?" I felt compelled to inquire.

"Well," she continued, "he was resting fitfully when a woman appeared at the door wanting to know how he was doing. [I'll call her Donna.] She had known the doctor for many years. We talked quietly for a few minutes. Your Dad must have heard us, because he opened his eyes and recognized the visitor. She approached the bed and they exchanged a few words. Just as she started to leave, your father spoke."

"Donna," your Dad whispered, "do you want to play a game of Scrabble?"

Some people might argue that he wasn't fully aware of his surroundings at that moment. Knowing Dad, though, the request was probably for real.

HOW COULD YOU!

Dad had a wonderful relationship with his sister, Evelyn. They were close during childhood, and as the years unfolded they and their spouses got together many times. Evelyn and Tom (McNaney) would travel down from Utica to visit Walter and Katherine, occasionally the reverse also happened. Evelyn had five children and Dad delivered the first three in Walton at Smith Hospital.

The relationship, though, was quite a typical one for siblings, i.e., not everything was roses.

One of Evelyn's children related the following story to me just a couple of years ago: As the story goes, Dad had just purchased a new car. I think it was in the 1930s before he married, so it was one of his first cars. He was quite proud of it and enjoyed showing it off. (He didn't know much about cars, but he knew what he liked!)

At any rate, Aunt Evelyn was pregnant and visiting Dad in Walton, anticipating a delivery within a few days. Dad just couldn't help himself: he had to give her a "tour" of the new vehicle, pointing out all of its special features. But more, he decided, was needed.

"How about a quick ride out into the country?" he eagerly asked his sister. "We won't go far. I want you to feel how smoothly it rides."

"All right, I guess. I'd be happy to take a 'brief' ride with you," came the cautious reply.

Off they went, down the paved road and then up and down some unpaved, dirt roads.... Needless to say, it was a little bumpier than either sibling expected. (This was the depression years and even the paved roads were a little rough.)

The bumpier it got, the more uncomfortable Evelyn became.

"Be careful, Walter. I don't want you to have to deliver the baby in the car."

"It will be fine," he answered somewhat indifferently. "Just relax."

Well, it wasn't fine, and she didn't relax. How could she? One of her worst fears materialized: on the return trip her "water" broke. Now it was obvious that the birth was hours not days away.

But my father, that "sensitive" physician, wasn't as concerned about his sister and the baby as he was about the condition of the new car.

"Evelyn," he nearly shouted. "You've ruined my new car seat. Just look at the mess you've created."

"But Walter," she answered firmly, "You didn't cover the seat. You weren't very prepared for this little ride."

He didn't need to be reminded of that oversight. He gritted his teeth and sped on home, hardly saying another word.

When they arrived back at the house, he jumped out, slammed the door, stormed away—leaving her still seated, waiting for a helping hand. It didn't come. She had to waddle up the stairs and into the house all by herself.

I'll bet I know who didn't clean up the car seat!

PARALYSIS

I was seventeen and proud of myself—a basketball star, reasonably good student, more mature, I thought, than most of my male contemporaries. I was busy in Dad's laboratory, the last room in the back of the medical office in our home. Dad had been teaching me how to do some simple lab tests—with blood or urine. I was diligently testing some urine for sugar levels, planning to finish up and skip out back to shoot some hoops on the court in the driveway. Dad was with a patient in the examining room just a few feet away. I could hear them talking.

I thought I heard my name called out. This was not unusual, since Dad was always bringing me in to help him or observe a procedure. The day before I had helped him hold someone's arm so he could put in some stitches. Nothing strange about hearing my name.

So, I put down my sample and walked down the short hallway to the examining room. I could see Dad working on a patient as I approached. He was sitting on a chair at the foot of the table. I stopped at his side, slightly behind him, and glanced at the patient.

I froze! I mean I couldn't move a muscle. I couldn't speak. I just stood there like a dope. You see, I had snuck up unawares on Dad's examination of a female patient, you know, in the private area of female anatomy. I knew that much, but I also realized I shouldn't be standing there staring.

Seconds dragged on and Dad hadn't yet even noticed me. I remember thinking "Why can't I back out of here?" Just as I opened my mouth to speak, the woman coughed, you know, the kind of what's-going-on? type of sound. Dad looked up at her face and followed her eyes to me.

"What are you doing in here, Bob?" he asked with a look that could kill on his face. "Get out, out," he demanded with a wave of his hand.

Robert J. Eells

Suddenly I found the strength to move. I backed out of the room, down the hallway, bumping into the fridge and almost falling backwards over a stool. I ended up sitting on the stool, trying to calm down and figure out what had just happened.

By the end of the day I had concluded that I wasn't as sophisticated as I had previously thought. I didn't share this insight with my buddies.

AT YOUR CONVENIENCE

How times have changed....

Several years ago I talked my Dad into getting rid of the drugs which were still located in his office. He had a small side room next to his desk where they were stored. And there were many drugs, of all kinds, even some prescription drugs— antibiotics and painkillers. Many years ago doctors could order them from drug companies and dispense them directly to patients as needed.

I emptied the drugs into several large bags which filled up my car trunk. I drove to the town dump, and after getting instructions on where to throw them, began my task.

This activity brought back memories of my Dad's office, especially what regularly happened in his waiting room. In recent months other former patients have also reminded me of what took place in that room.

Picture this: a room full of patients waiting to see the doctor. There were seven chairs, four facing three, and as you entered from the street you could see a stand upon which rested a small black and white TV. The office door opens and at the same moment the phone rings. Doc Eells motions the next patient to come in and sit down beside his desk as he picks up the phone and begins talking. The door remains slightly ajar so you can overhear the following conversation:

"Sounds like that antibiotic isn't working very well. I'll change the prescription and put it out for you in the usual place. Pick it up on your way home. It will have directions on the label."

The usual place? Where was that? Answer: on top of the TV! When the person arrived in the late afternoon he or she would simply open the door, approach the TV, examine the several bottles on top, and pick out the right one. If the doctor was in, payment would be made; if not, a bill would come later.

How times have changed....

105

OF COURSE I DO

The doctor dressed quickly and wolfed down his breakfast. The surgery was set for 8:00 a.m. He loved just about every aspect of general practice, well, apart from autopsies: he preferred to work on <u>live</u> patients. He knew he was a lucky man, moreover, because unlike most GP's he owned a small hospital. Second floor contained the surgery, and this room had become a rather busy one, with many kinds of "minor" operations taking place there. Tonsils, appendixes, and cysts could be removed, hips had to be pinned, broken bones reset, an occasional Caesarean "ripped" a newborn into the world.

He finished breakfast just as the kids arrived for a few bites before heading off to school. Though he had prepared his own breakfast, the Mrs. was now on hand to ensure that the children had a proper beginning to their day. He crossed the street, again not paying much attention to the traffic, entered Smith Hospital, and headed straight for his office. He examined the patient's chart to confirm that the paperwork was in order and that all the indications were still "green." By now, he realized, the patient had been prepped and was already in the operating room, ready for sedation.

After talking briefly with the patient and giving the nurse instructions about the anesthesia, he stepped into the side room to clean thoroughly before being gowned up by a second nurse. Midway through this process, he was joined by his associate, Dr. Wilbur, who quickly repeated the same routine. He and Harry had been assisting one another for many years. It had been a congenial relationship. They talked about the morning procedure but also about whatever popped into their minds.

This morning it was a gallbladder that had to be removed. Together they had performed this operation many times and expected few, if any, surprises.

No problems for the first forty-five minutes. The incision was perfect, vessels had been clamped, and nothing "inappropriate" had been cut, damaged, or ignored. By now the banter was about everything but the gallbladder.

"There it is," Doc Eells noted. "Right where it should be."

"Bingo," replied Harry. "Let's take a closer look. Ouch, it's a mess. From its appearance, I'd say it hasn't been working properly for a long time."

Doc Eells agreed and they proceeded to excise the offending organ.

Then something usual appeared.

"Where's that bleeding coming from?" Doc Eells queried.

"I don't know, we haven't nicked anything important as far as I can tell," replied Dr. Wilbur.

No more idle banter now as they focused all their attention on the emerging crisis. They dabbed and suctioned and probed, but to no avail.

"Doctors," interrupted the nurse who was observing the vital signs, "His blood pressure is dropping rapidly. Surely, he's not losing that much blood."

She was right. Blood loss was significant but not in a volume to cause such a sharp decline in blood pressure. Something else must be wrong.

They went to work, trying everything they knew to stem the loss and raise the pressure—more fluids were given, changes were made in the anesthetic, every effort was expended to solve the mystery. Nothing seemed to work.

"Pressure is still plunging, doctors, it shouldn't be allowed to drop much lower!"

"Walter, what's next? What can we do?" Dr. Wilbur implored.

"I don't know, Harry, we're trying everything. We don't have much time!"

Everything? Everything? What have I missed, he wondered to himself. I can't lose this patient. I just can't!

Then he awoke, rolled over and looked at the clock: it read 6:05 a.m. Dreaming again, in fact, the same dream over and over: He and Harry getting stuck with a problem that seemed unsolvable. Sometimes a gallbladder, sometimes exploring for cancer, always something big and perplexing. Strange? Maybe not, he thought, but he didn't like to fail. He rarely did. Why can't the dreams have a happier ending?

The above is a true story, because one day when Dad was 95 I asked him if he ever dreamed at night and this was what he told me. I smiled when he shared it with me. A perfect dream for him, except for the ending.

HELLO THERE

I'm sitting across from my parents at their favorite restaurant, T.A.'s. My sister is with us. Shortly before heading home, we've discussed the likelihood that we won't have too many more opportunities to share with them these precious moments. We've done this so many times in recent years: Mom decided several years ago that she had cooked enough meals and set enough tables for a lifetime. We both agree.

The ritual is always the same. They arrive, wave or nod to a few regulars, check out the menu, though they usually select from the same three or four options. Mom and Dad will order something "simple," and request it to be served on two separate plates. So many times I've heard her say: "They give such big portions here; I can't possibly eat that much."

Then we settle back and relax. Eleanor and I cherish this time together. We talk about many things, though Dad can't catch it all because of his hearing loss, and Mom wants to stay "positive," so we don't complain about politics or religion. Regardless, it's a wonderful and precious feeling sitting here.

When both half portions are consumed, another ritual begins. Mom asks Dad if he wants dessert. Sometimes he's in the mood, sometimes not. In either case, Mom will do her duty, dessert being the favorite part of her meal. We joke with her about one obvious point—she never shares with anyone. We all laugh, except Mom, who doesn't see the humor.

For Eleanor and me, one of the highlights of the restaurant experience happens when customers stop by to greet our parents. We've never failed to witness this part of the ritual. Today, several people drop by on their way in or out of the restaurant. Most seem to be former patients, but a few are just regulars who enjoy visiting with Mom and Dad.

Today, however, is even more unique. An older couple approach our table. I glance their way and think husband and wife? or mother and son? As they stand beside the table, it's clear that the latter is the case.

"Hello, Dr. Eells," the woman says with a broad smile. "Do you remember me?" She states her name and repeats the question a little louder.

Dad laughs and confesses, "I honestly can't recall. I'm getting pretty forgetful of late."

The woman isn't offended. She puts her hand on her partner's shoulder and says, "This is my son. He was one of your first babies. You delivered him in 1930, shortly after you arrived in Walton. Can you remember his birth?" With some embarrassment Dad can't. They all find some humor in the situation and agree that aging can damage our memories, even the milestones.

I'm sitting back in my chair and marveling at the whole interaction. It's "living history" right before my eyes. It's 1993 and Dad helped usher this older gentleman into the world sixty-three years ago! Where has the time gone, I think, where...?

WHAT'S IN A NAME?

It was May 1976. I was excited about the events surrounding the upcoming weekend. Finally, I had finished my work for the Ph.D. in American Studies at the University of New Mexico. Soon I would be marching down the platform in my new robe, with three stripes on each sleeve designating my "lofty" status. On the platform I would be introduced by the Provost, my graduate professor, Dr. Joel Jones. He would then give me my new hood, shake my hand, and send me off into the world of academia.

My excitement was enhanced by the presence of my parents who had flown all the way in from New York State. In my mind I still could recreate the day my father had learned that an M.D. was not in my future. What a terribly disappointed and sad look he had given me. No son to work with him and no one to carry on his practice after he retired. But now, in 1976, he would at least get to witness the bestowing of an earned doctorate on his son. Not a medical degree but a terminal degree, nonetheless, allowing me to teach at the college level. My hopes were high for the day.

It began on the right note. My parents were staying with me and Janice at the home of Janice's parents, Milton and Esther Johnson. Everyone got along well: it was a time of good cheer, pleasant conversation, and, as usual, beautiful Albuquerque weather.

The afternoon of the ceremony arrived, and we traveled to the auditorium where my parents, wife, and in-laws found seats in the balcony. During the program, I turned several times to my right, seeking their location. I finally spotted them high up near the top.

Most of the program was mundane. Blah, Blah, Blah, opined the guest speaker, the former governor of New Mexico. Things began to move rather quickly, though, when he finished. Ph.D. candidates would be recognized first—individually. (The vast number of undergraduates would be acknowledged as a group, by majors.) About forty doctoral candidates rose when the moment arrived, and we worked our way around to the side of the platform, waiting our turn by the steps. Because of my last name, I was to be one of the first names called.

I was excited, especially for my father. The Provost ran through the list and performed the necessary rituals. I was next. He looked at his list, glanced down at me and gave me the smile of familiarity. I was ready.

He called out my name, for everyone to hear: "Conferring the Ph.D. in American Studies to Robert James Eells." I hesitated in mid-step, for he had just committed a cardinal sin in my family—pronouncing "Eells" as "Ells," emphasizing the "lls" not the "ees!" I couldn't believe my ears. Dr. Jones had been my professor and was someone with whom I had had numerous conversations. How could he have done this?

I somehow made my way across the stage, turned and let him drape me with the new hood. As I turned back to shake his hand, I whispered, "it's Eells, not Eells."

"Sorry, Bob," he whispered back. "That's what I thought it was, but the graduate office insisted otherwise." Great, I thought, just great.

After the ceremony my wife pulled me aside and asked, "Did Joel say what I thought he said?"

"Yes," I replied unhappily. "Did Dad mention it?"

He hadn't mentioned it, she answered. And he never did, at least to me. But I'll bet he was disappointed. His son's one big moment in the sun, and they got it wrong.

Dad, however, did have one consolation—he got to address me as "Dr." every time he sent me a letter or postcard, for the next twenty-four years!

I hope that I make him proud of the Eells name.

O DANNY BOY

In an earlier edition I related how my mother tricked my father into traveling by plane for the first time. That was in the mid-1960s. In subsequent years he became very comfortable with flying, and they winged it all around the world, literally. They made it, for example, to New Zealand and to Australia and visited Europe several times (even the former Soviet Union where mother sneaked in good Christian literature!). One of their favorite locations, however, was Northern Ireland. They toured Ulster on three occasions—1982, 1986, and 1990. The primary lure was international conferences of the Reformed Presbyterian Church, but they also had time for side trips throughout Northern Ireland, England, and Scotland. One of their favorite hosts was George Wright and his wife, Ann. What follows is my recreation of an e-mail message sent by George to my cousin, Beverly McCready.

It seems that on their first trip in 1982 Mom and Dad decided to break off from the main group of visitors and hop over to England. George agreed to transport them by car to the train station in Londonderry. They would then travel to Belfast and to London.

What my parents didn't realize, however, was that at the same time a "loyalist" celebration was just ending in Londonderry. When they entered the train it was beginning to fill up—with rowdy young men, many of whom were "under the influence," if you get the drift.

My Mother, bless her, was like a charter member of the Women's Christian Temperance Union. Alcohol and drunkenness were evils to her, plain and simple. (She professed throughout most of her life that total abstinence had been her practice, but did once admit sipping from a glass of wine in Italy in a moment of weakness: "It tasted like dishwater," was her dismissal.)

113

At any rate, at first the distinguished couple thought they were alone. Not for long. Before the train departed several young men stumbled into the carriage—singing, joking, and belching, and maybe a few other pleasantries.

I can see it clearly in my mind, the rather different responses: Mom a little pale, staring at her hands and handbag, fidgeting, no doubt wondering if there wasn't someplace else to sit; Dad settling back, putting a toothpick in his mouth and reaching for his latest paperback novel. (His concern was better hidden.)

Mom's worst fears became reality when the young men discovered them, especially when they realized Americans were in their midst. The decibel level rose even higher along with the somewhat incoherent babble.

Then two events took place which no doubt drained more blood from Mom's face and perhaps even caused the toothpick to drop from my Dad's lips. First, one man got so excited that he somehow pushed himself upright and began to wave his arms around until one of them plunged through the glass in the door, scattering pieces everywhere. He was cut but not severely, and Doc Eells, uncharacteristically, kept quiet about his "profession."

The second event was even more "shocking." A red-haired man got so carried away by his love for America and this adorable couple that he lurched forward without warning, threw his arms around Mom, and gave her a big kiss! (By now she probably looked like an albino.) One can only imagine what was going on in my mother's mind, or my father's for that matter.

Somehow they survived the trip, this "eventful" journey, as Dad described it briefly in a subsequent letter to George. And, amazingly, they came back for more—in 1986 (when George received the full details from Dad) and again four years later. Sounds like they were both habitual travelers by the 1980s, a couple who would let very little stand in the way of further adventures.

NOT EASILY OVERCOME

The above is the Eells family motto. Dad was the incarnation of this slogan. Little seemed to deter him from setting and reaching his goals.

Even at 95, after his heart attack, he ploughed ahead—literally. I can close my eyes and see him groaning and pushing himself up from his easy chair in the living room, walking, almost charging, ahead toward the office or kitchen. What a sight! This little old man, barely 115 pounds, abandoning the group, oblivious to everything except his objective.

"Hold on, Doc, let me catch up," would be the "desperate" plea from the home-care helper. She was in a bind because of the oxygen tubing hanging from his nose. He ignored it but she couldn't, meaning she had to unwind it, keep him from tripping over it as he walked, and make sure that he and this snake would arrive at the destination together without a major catastrophe. In addition, all kinds of obstacles stood in his way. He simply brushed them aside—using his cane which was supposed to provide support but usually trailed behind him like a tail.

"Dad," I would call out, "use the cane for balance."

"I don't need it," he would reply with some annoyance. (Actually, I had to say it twice because of his poor hearing.)

He would arrive at his office, call me in, and proceed to discuss, excitedly, some issue relating to the next Eells family bulletin or some item concerning the monthly budget. Then he would get up and we would repeat everything all over again as he headed for another room.

Such determination kept him going. Combined with God's grace, it gave him the energy to reach the age of 97. We were doubly blessed.

DOCTOR TO THE POOR

The above title comes from a comment by a regular correspondent to the *Walton Reporter* upon hearing of Dad's death. It made me think of all the confirmations I have received over the years about his undeniably "fair" prices and his wonderful generosity. Here are just a few examples:

—reading from a touching letter by a former patient, Janith Kilpatrick, who sent the following note on Dad's ninetieth birthday: "We saved all the bills from you and Smith Hospital when our five kids where born and have given them to each one when their first arrived. What an impression! They were amazed at the change [in the cost] in just their lifetime." By the time of Dad's last delivery in the late 1970s, I recall, his prices had "escalated" all the way up to $150!

—listening to pharmacist Bill Hastings as he pulled me aside about ten years ago with this special recollection: From time to time, he informed me, Dad would wander into the pharmacy, seemingly just for idle conversation. Then after a few minutes the doctor would say: "Bill, you know _____? Well, he'll be coming in soon to pick up a prescription I've given him. He doesn't really have the money right now." Doc Eells would then take out his wallet, inquire about the price, and pay for the drug himself. "Just tell him it's all taken care of, Bill." It's all taken care of…

—sitting on a stool in Dad's office in the mid-1980s, remembering my last visit to a doctor in the Chicago suburbs. I realized Dad was still seeing patients, in fact, several had been through that very day. Just for comparison, I asked: "Dad, what do you charge for an office visit today?"

"$12," he answered. "I've had to raise the price in recent years. I didn't want to, but my costs have risen, too." It's still a good deal, I thought to myself.

—glancing with astonishment at a bill I stumbled upon while cleaning out my parents' home. It seems that a long-time friend and patient, Charles Michel, had been under Dad's care in September 1946. In particular, surgery had been performed on Charles at Smith Hospital, requiring a sojourn of one week. Here are the specifics:

Aug. 27—Sept. 3 (7 days @ $5.00)	$35.00
Operating room service	10.00
Anesthetic	10.00
Total	$55.00
Insurance	-38.00
Balance due	$16.50

I realize that this comes from 1946. But it appears to me more like charges one would expect from 1846!

—reviewing an audio tape which revealed Dad's approach to accepting payment for services rendered. As the story goes, Dad delivered a baby to a young couple who had recently arrived in Walton. Approximately one week after giving birth, the new mother came to the office with the total amount in cash—$150. As Dad took the money and glanced down at his accounting book, he said with a wink: "Now look what you've done. You've messed up my figures. It's only $50, didn't you know?" He knew they were just starting out and had very little money. The woman left with tears in her eyes and $100 in her pocket.

—remembering my father's frustration involving money after his heart attack in December 1997. My sister and I insisted that he and Mom had to secure round-the-clock care help if they wished to continue living in their house. They agreed, but in only a few weeks Dad realized how much this was costing—help plus benefits reaching many thousands of dollars per month. They had a comfortable monthly income, but he was still distressed, because he loved supporting his family, friends, church, and his numerous charities. After all the new expenses, however, there was "not enough money left to give away," I

overhead him lament.   That was one of his greatest
disappointments during the last two years of his life.

Not enough money left to give away—a decent legacy for
any man or woman.

COINCIDENCE?

My cousin, Barb Thurnau, and her husband, Carl, were on their way to Walton to pay their respects shortly after Dad's passing. It was a chilly January day with snow on the ground, as they approached Masonville, a few miles down the road from Walton. As they pulled out of this small town, they approached a car on the side of the road. Its hood was up in the classic sign of trouble, and a man was beside it looking cold and forlorn. Being good Samaritans, they just couldn't ignore this stranger.

Carl parked in front of the disabled vehicle to see if he could help. He got out and walked toward the man. "Won't start?" came the sympathetic question.

"No," replied the stranger. "I've been working at it for quite awhile. I guess the battery's dead. I should have changed it before now. I'll walk back up to town; it's not far."

"Hold on," interrupted Carl, gesturing toward his car. "We'll give you a ride back. You look cold enough for one day."

The man happily accepted the offer and they piled into the car whose heater was working wonderfully. After brief introductions, Carl turned around and headed back to Masonville. A few moments later, the rider asked what the Thurnau's were doing in this neck of the woods.

"We're headed to Walton," Barb noted. "My uncle passed away a couple of days ago and we're headed that way to show our support to the family. Are you from around here?"

"Yes, I'm a local," said the man.

"Well, then, perhaps you knew my uncle. His name was Dr. Walter Eells, a Walton physician for many years. Does that name ring a bell?"

The man flinched and quickly smiled from ear to ear. "Know him," he laughed excitedly, "he delivered me and all my children!" [Of course he did.]

· For a short time they all shared more laughter and memories. Later Barb and Carl reflected on this event and concluded that it probably wasn't so unique—this was Delaware County after all. The name "Eells" would no doubt have been on many hearts and minds during those particular days.

SYMPATHY?

The boy was having a good time playing outside. He wasn't getting into mischief or picking on his sister, just horsing around with a couple of buddies. It was, in every sense, a typical summer day in Walton.

He forgot about the warning from his mother. A boy has to play, doesn't he? So, they turned the old shed into their fort, as they had done so many times before. Lost in his imaginary struggle to survive against another Indian attack, something else—very real—struck first. Not a very big enemy but a potentially deadly one, nonetheless.

"Ouch," he cried while hiding in a corner waiting for the battle to commence. What was that? Did he back into a nail? Was it some kind of farm tool? The pain came from his left shoulder which he felt gingerly. Then it happened again in the back of his neck. Suddenly, he realized what had occurred: stung by a bee, not once but twice. Now he remembered his mother's repeated warning: "Son, you're allergic to bees. Being stung is a very serious matter. Stay away from bees, please!"

He bolted out of the shed, running toward the house. His playmates followed, confused and frightened by the victim's screaming. By the time his mother had rushed him to the car and was backing out of the driveway, he was already feeling lightheaded and breathing with difficulty. He thought he heard his Mom say something about going to the family doctor, but he wasn't sure—about anything.

Mom tore through town in a matter of minutes, coming to a screeching halt in front of Doc Eells' office. She picked up her son and carried him in. It was about 6:00 p.m. and the doctor was eating dinner with his family. She carried him past a couple of startled patients sitting in the waiting room, pushed open the door into the formal dining room and called out:

"Dr. Eells," are you back there? My boy has been stung by a bee and I'm afraid he's going into shock. Can you see him? Now?"

The doctor could, of course, and they both hurried back into the examining room. She was right. The boy was going into shock. He was pale, with shallow breathing, and a rapid heart beat. Immediate action was called for. The key procedure was a shot—or shots—to counteract the poison and the body's natural reaction to it.

Doc Eells administered the first shot, gave the boy some oxygen, and hovered over him trying to think of something else to do. After a few minutes of nervous attention, the boy appeared not to be responding.

"I'm doing all I can," he whispered to the distraught mother, "but we may lose him." She looked a little faint herself, so he pulled up a chair so she could sit beside the examining table. From there she held her son's hand and caressed his face.

Another shot was given and a third. Minutes dragged on. Thirty minutes seemed like an eternity. But it worked: the boy's color began to return, his breathing became less labored, and his heart rate returned to the normal range. By the end of the hour the crisis was over. Doctor and mother breathed a sigh of relief.

Later in the evening the mother retold the exciting drama to her husband and a few neighbors. She heaped praise on the doctor, his medical instincts, and his obvious concern for the son's condition.

"He was as upset as I was," she summarized the event. That may well be true, thought the boy overhearing the re-creation. But all he remembered was the last few minutes in the doctor's office. What stuck in his mind, as they had readied themselves to leave, was the kindly doctor's pronouncement: "You realize, young man, you've interrupted my dinner!" Was he kidding? Probably.

COMPASSIONATE TRICKSTER

Long-time patient Dave Adams shared this story with me at the church after Dad's funeral.

At a certain point in his childhood Dave was very sick. He remembers the pain and discomfort like it was yesterday. He had difficulty breathing and holding down his food. Years later his parents recounted to him that they were afraid he might not make it—partly because Doc Eells was honest with his own assessment. It didn't look good to anyone.

Soon young Dave was admitted to Smith Hospital for intensive care. He wasn't thrilled about being there nor about the fact that his doctor wanted to give him a shot.

Shortly after Dave arrived, the family doctor entered the room and calmly explained the situation to him. "You need this shot, David," he declared. "It will help and put you on the road to recovery."

Like most children, Dave wasn't fond of needles. His demeanor made this quite clear to the doctor.

"Look, David, I'll make you a partner with me in giving the shot," said the doctor, bending slightly down toward the young patient.

"What do you mean?" came the reply, with a little hint of new interest.

"Well, I can give this shot with any one of three needle sizes—small, medium, or large. I'll bring in the box containing all three and then let you examine them and decide which one I'll use."

Actually, Dave thought, that sounded fair enough. If he had to get a shot at least he had some say in the matter.

Doc Eells turned and left the room. In a few moments he returned—with a box. The box was opened and, indeed, it did contain three needles of varying sizes. Dave pretended to examine them thoroughly, knowing, of course, what his ultimate choice would be.

A moment later he announced: "I'll take this one," pointing to the smallest object.

"Good choice," the doctor agreed. "I would choose that one too."

Doc Eells then turned around facing away from his patient, rummaged through the box, making a few medical noises. He picked up a little bottle from the table with his left hand, holding it out just far enough for Dave to see it. Still with his back to Dave, he brought together bottle and needle. Using his left hand he wiped Dave's upper arm with a little piece of white cotton.

"Turn your head away from the arm, David, so you don't have to watch. It will be a little easier on you."

Dave started to look away, but before the move was even completed, he felt the pain. Ouch, it hurt! Glancing quickly back toward the spot it hurt even more, at least emotionally. He couldn't believe his eyes: Doc Eells was separating a needle from the syringe—a very big needle! He had been tricked, but good. Before he even had a chance to complain, the doctor departed.

But this is not the end of Dave's story. You see, this shot was just the beginning. The regimen called for shots every four hours for several days, night and day. Dave didn't mention the size of the needles for subsequent shots. But he did conclude, emotionally, by saying:

"Bob, your Dad gave the shots, all of them. Even during the night. A nurse could have given some of them, but he insisted on giving them all."

Of course he did, I thought, hoping the lump in my throat wouldn't prevent me from further conversation.

SECURITY

My tummy hurts. Bad. It has been hurting for a long time. I thought the hurt would go away. But it hasn't. Mommy says my tummy gets upset once in awhile and not to worry about it. But I do.

Yesterday she and Daddy were in my bedroom checking on me. Daddy put something in my mouth and told me to keep it under my tongue. He's a doctor, you know, so this is probably what doctors do. Then he stuck me with a big needle. I didn't like that one bit. I wonder why he wanted my blood?

Later, I hear them talking outside my room, kind of in whispers. They must be talking about me.

This morning Daddy came into the room and said he had a surprise for me. I would get a special visit to the big white house across the street. I don't get there very often. Mommy thinks I'm not old enough to cross the street. I think my Daddy works there in that big house. He works here too.

Now Daddy is smiling and talking about this special day. He picks me up and holds me close to him. He's carrying me down the stairs, across the street, into the white house. My tummy still hurts, but Daddy laughs and says the visit will make me feel better. Mommy is there too, holding my hand.

Daddy puts me on a bed and some ladies in white are all around me. There's that needle again. I haven't even had my visit yet. I'm really getting sleepy. Will Daddy get mad if I take a nap?

My tummy still hurts. There's a big Band-Aid on my tummy. The ladies in white don't want me to touch it.

Daddy is in the room. It's a big room and the people are here too. He says everything is fine. Soon, the hurt will go away. In a few days I'll be as good as new. I'll bet he's right. He'll make the hurt go away. He does that, you know—he makes people feel better. I'm sleepy again. Can't wait to start running and playing. Soon, I'll be in school. If they have playtime, I think I'll like school. Thanks, Daddy.

I'M THE BOSS!

In the Eells' house Sunday was the Sabbath, and it was not a secular day. That was Mom's belief and commitment. One consequence of this stance meant no TV on the Lord's Day. I must admit cheating a little on the Sabbath—by sneaking downstairs to watch (silently) baseball games on "Sunday" afternoon. I watched them in the office waiting room to minimize my chances of being caught.

Dad didn't object much, until two things happened: 1) we got our first color set (1960), and 2) we discovered what color did to our favorite western, Bonanza.

My siblings and I put tremendous pressure on Mom to bend her rule a little. After all, Bonanza didn't start until after the evening service at church, and it was a great family show. We pleaded, but Mom held her ground.

Finally, Dad intervened. Out of the blue, it seemed, he announced before the whole family: "Mother, I bought this TV and I'll decide whether or not to watch Bonanza!" (Yeh, Dad, we silently cheered.) Mom said nothing, merely turned around and left the room.

We watched Bonanza from that day forward. After a few weeks, Mom joined us—pretending not to watch as she enjoyed her late night snack of cookies and ice cream.

COMFORT ZONE

I'm riding in the car in the back seat next to the window. Kenny is in the middle and Eleanor is beside him. It's late at night and we're heading back from the Henderson farm after dinner. Mom is driving, of course, and Dad is in front of me, with a toothpick in his mouth.

It's dark and I'm sleepy. Can hardly keep my eyes open. I hear Mom and Dad talking, but it sounds funny—like they're far away. I can't quite make out what they're talking about. It doesn't matter. I know I'm loved. They take care of us. How do kids survive without parents like mine?

A bump jars me awake. I'll head upstairs for some serious sleep. Tomorrow awaits. So does the future.

MY ACHING BACK

I was home on a summer break from college. It was mid-afternoon, and I was napping upstairs in my bedroom. Thanks to college, I had rediscovered the joys of afternoon naps. I wasn't fast asleep because I heard my parents talking in the kitchen. I realized I was in trouble when Dad asked Mom, "Do you know where Bob is?" In a moment the kitchen door opened and Dad called out: "R. J., are you up there? I need some help at the hospital. Can you come down?"

"Sure," I answered without much enthusiasm.

When I reached the kitchen, I got the bad news: "Bob," said Dad, "we're full again across the street. Can you put up a bed in the second floor hallway?"

"No problem," I responded without much enthusiasm, for this was not one of my favorite jobs. I crossed Townsend Street, entered the hospital, and worked my way up to the third floor attic. That's where the bed frames were stored. I found the right pile of equipment and paused, hoping somehow to gain some additional strength for the task at hand.

You see, I faced two problems. First, the bed frames were cast iron and felt like a ton. In reality, they were probably more like a hundred pounds, but I could barely lift them, nonetheless.

Second, I had to drag it carefully across the floor and then down the steep, narrow passageway to the second floor. I had to proceed step-by-step, holding on for dear life, praying that I didn't lose my grip and allow the frame to plunge straight down to the hallway. Such a catastrophe would result in either digging a big hole in the second floor or eliminating a nurse or patient (or visitor) who was in the wrong place at the wrong time.

Feeling immensely sorry for myself, I somehow managed—as I had done many times before—to guide the frame down the stairs. I then returned to the attic and repeated the trip two more times—bringing down the heavy foot and head boards. A nurse helped me assemble the monster. I tried not to reflect on the fact

129

that she was half my size and would never have been able to transport this monster down from the attic. I still felt sorry for myself.

I thought about the patient soon to inhabit this bed. Hope he or she experiences the healing power of my father or Dr. Wilbur and lingers for a couple of extra days just to be safe, I mused. Lingering would give me a break, for as soon as the patient recovered or another bed opened up elsewhere, I would have to repeat the entire process in reverse. Again, not my favorite job.

No such luck this time. The very next day a bed opened up, and the patient was moved. I got the news the following afternoon. Dad took it all in stride. But I got to feel sorry for myself all over again.

REGRETS

One of the TV shows Dad and I occasionally watched together in the 1950s was The Naked City. It was about life in New York City, mostly human interest stories. We enjoyed it because there was a minimum of violence and it focused in on ordinary people facing different situations. I can still hear the announcer saying at the end of each segment, "there are eight million stories in the naked city—this has been one of them."

The ending makes me think of all the stories about my father which I witnessed or heard but didn't jot down so they wouldn't be forgotten. This is my only regret, since there are many more to be told about this country doctor. As time goes on, I'll remember more—perhaps enough for another edition. If the readers have some to share with me, it will make further efforts even more likely and more rewarding.

* * * *

I will remember him—forever.

SNAPSHOTS

My mind is filled with these memories and with the recollections of other individuals, some pleasant, some less so:

Dad was proud of the fact that he never lost a patient in the operating room due to his error or as a result of infection because of carelessness in dressing wounds. He did, however, lose one patient in his office in the mid-1950s. A male patient arrived who required an antibiotic as a precaution after a wound had been closed and bandaged. Dad asked him if he was allergic to penicillin. He didn't think so. To check, Dad squirted a little directly unto his eyelid and a few moments later the eye looked normal. A shot of penicillin was given, and shortly later the man collapsed in the office, apparently from a reaction to the drug. Efforts to revive him were unsuccessful. This death, naturally, was a tragedy for all concerned—but since it occurred in Walton fifty years ago, no one sued!

* * * * *

Rev. Joe Hill recalls a time in the 1950s, when Doc Eells wanted him to drive him to a house in the country where an "accident" had occurred. When they arrived, it was immediately apparent that it was a shooting, in fact, a suicide. A woman had been depressed and taken her own life by placing a shotgun so that when discharged it fired directly into her head. "It was a big mess. You don't ever want to see anything like that, Bob," Joe concluded sadly. Even in a small town, a country doctor will see just about everything.

* * * * *

Can you picture Walter Eells getting a speeding ticket? Well, maybe you can, at least before getting married to Katherine—who quickly assumed the family driving responsibilities. Rummaging through Dad's scrapbooks, I found proof of his malfeasance: placed there for all to see is the newspaper clipping showing W.E. Eells being stopped for speeding and being issued a ticket for a $2.00 fine. Who knows, perhaps Mrs. E. saved him from becoming a serial speeder.

* * * * *

Do you have this image, as I did, that Walter Eells must have been an "A" student in college and medical school? Wrong. Once again the scrapbook shows the real academic truth: grades ranging from D to A. In fact, he was even on probation for one semester at Cornell. Like many students, he did well in subjects he found interesting and less well in subjects he found irrelevant. He loved biology, for example, and hated psychology. Concerning the latter, he once confessed to me: "I found psychology boring. I could barely keep awake in class. I wanted to study the human body, not some crazy (Freudian?) ideas about human motivation." That does sound like Dad.

* * * * *

Can you see the shy teenager in a high school play? I couldn't—until I discovered a brochure describing a 1916 Walton production. It was December so Dad was fourteen years old. He played Puck (or Robin Goodfellow) in Shakespeare's Midsummer Night's Dream. The "mischievous" Puck is the description of Dad's role in the synopsis. Don't you wish there had been videotape back then? What a treat it would be.

* * * * *

Can you see Dad as a ten-year-old, sitting in the old Opera House in Walton, watching with fascination as a presidential candidate worked the crowd? It was 1912, and the candidate was Teddy Roosevelt, running on his third-party ticket against

Taft and Wilson. "He put on quite a show," is how Dad remembered the performance. Dad was probably the last Waltonian alive to have seen Teddy Roosevelt.

* * * *

You might think that Walter Eells is an uncommon name. It probably is, since the last name is rare enough. How many Walter Eelles are there? Who knows? Probably not many. What are the chances of seeing three together at the same time? People who are familiar with the Walton Eelles might answer— that's easy: Doc, his nephew and grandnephew. They would be right, of course, and these three were together many times.

What about the possibility, though, of even more Walters meeting at the same time? How about four, five, even six? Well, unlikely as it may seem, six did gather together, thanks to the work of my father.

It happened in the late 1980s. Dad was planning the annual Eells reunion for Walton and suddenly came up with the idea of writing to several other Walters. He knew they existed. He had practically memorized the Eells family history book. So, he went to work and contacted three Walters who had never attended. All lived in the East, but a couple were hundreds of miles away. It worked. They accepted and all arrived at the Masonville Inn several miles down the road from Walton. It was a beautiful August day and the newcomers mingled with distant cousins, taking pleasure in the fact that they were no doubt making "history." Eells history. Six Walter Eelles at the same place on the same day.

My father loved that day. The smile rarely left his face.

* * * * *

I was a big Brooklyn Dodgers fan. When the Dodgers finally won the World Series in 1955—against the hated Yankees—I was eleven years old. I went crazy, jumping around the house, shouting for joy. I can still see the smile on my father's face when he and Mom tried to calm me down. "It's just a game, Bob," he said matter-of-factly. Later in the day I heard them chuckling about my long-lasting excitement. Later in life I realized how much I was like my father—my excitement about teaching resembling his love for medicine.

CAROLYN DELLWO'S SNAPSHOTS

[Carolyn is Dad's niece, daughter of Evelyn (Eells) McNaney.]

In the winter of 1952, in my senior year at SU School of Nursing, I had a bad case of mononucleosis and had to take about six weeks leave from clinical studies to recuperate. Your folks invited me to come visit during that time and I remember staying out at the "cottage" as it then was. Towards the end of my stay when I was feeling better, your Dad asked me if I would like to scrub with him on a gallbladder surgery at Smith Hospital. Of course I was thrilled at the chance! Having just finished my "OR" (operating room) rotation, I had decided this was the specialty I wanted to pursue. I was used to the largeness of a big teaching hospital and to having rows of suture material of various sizes lined up on the instrument tray well in advance, just in case the surgeon might ask for it. I guess I must have looked skeptical at the rather scarce supply Uncle Doc had provided me and asked for more. He sternly reminded me that this wasn't Memorial Hospital and he didn't break out sterile sutures until and unless he needed them! I meekly agreed and the surgery, as I recall, went very smoothly. I have always remembered that day with pride, and regret that we didn't get to do it again. Marriage and motherhood put my OR career on hold shortly after that.

* * * * *

Perhaps you're not aware of the story of how mother helped your Dad through medical school by sending him money every month. She graduated from nursing school about the time he entered medical school in Albany. She went to work at the hospital in Seneca Falls, where she later met my Dad [Tom McNaney]. She made a commitment to send him a certain sum every month to help with his room and board. I think it was all of $50, which was a great deal in those days. She and Dad put off getting married for 3-4 years till he graduated. She never spoke of it as a hardship, but rather with great pride that she had been able to help him. And she always said he more than repaid her over the years, delivering three of us children, for instance, and in many other countless ways. But they always had a great affection for one another and kept in close touch. One picture I really treasure was taken less than two months before Mom died. We knew Mom had terminal cancer and had moved in with Barbara. I was up for a visit and Eleanor and Sharon drove your folks up for a few hours' visit one day. Mom was feeling good that day and they had a good time together and Sharon took some delightful pictures of Mom and your Dad, heads together and laughing, that are very special.

ADDENDA

Correspondence and tributes—general

Over the years my father received many notes, commendations, and letters of congratulations. What follows is just a small sampling of such messages.

1. Handwritten letter from a child, Thomas Jump

Hello. My name is Thomas Jump. I am learning about apples and I was hoping you could answer some questions for me. Is it true that "an apple a day keeps the doctor away"? Why do people say this? Are apples good for you? Thank you for your help.

2. Letter from Walton Central High School basketball team—1962 (minus RJE)

Dear Dr. and Mrs. Walter Eells

The members of the Varsity Team of Walton Central School wish to extend their deepest thanks and appreciation for the delicious meal that you sponsored.

We all appreciate your interest in our team.

Sincerely,

Tom Good, Don Price, Steve Gruver, Phil Kehr, Joe Carpenter, Thomas Evans, Bob Miller, Mac MacNaught, Terrell Roe, Paul Eaton, Bob Popp

3. Poem by Beverly (Henderson) McCready

The Lord had you there at my beginning, to catch my little frame.

The Lord had you there to take my tonsils out, when I thought it wasn't fair.

The Lord had you there when my big brother broke his toe, my sister her nose and my younger brother cut his finger.

The Lord had you there, 10 years later to catch another little frame, my sister, Linda, whose unexpected presence never was explained!

The Lord had you there when our Dad suffered a heart attack and then at his side there you stood when the Lord said, "No Walter, it's time for him to come home for good and not look back."

Dear Uncle, God has given you gifts and blessed you in so many ways, used you in so many lives and how we do thank God for you on this very special day!

4. Poem celebrating Dad's 80th birthday

THE REMARKABLE DR. EELLS

Most buildings today, you know
Are named for many "Big Wheels"
And we, of course, have ours—
The "Remarkable Dr. Eells."

He's been on many school boards—
Involved with many big deals
The man that we honor tonight
The "Remarkable Dr. Eells."

He went to Cornell, Albany and Binghamton
To study how a sick person feels
And he's gone on healing for years and years—
The "Remarkable Dr. Eells."

To find his ancestors in Europe
He went to churches, cemeteries and jails
But he won't tell us where he found them
The "Remarkable Dr. 'Ails'."

For years he has made home movies,
Turned out hundred of reels
His wife says, "He deserves an Oscar"
This "Remarkable Dr. Eells."

This Saturday's his birthday
No need asking how he feels
He thinks he's good for 80 more
The "Remarkable Dr. Eells."

And there's no truth to the story
That in meetings his head slowly keels
Cause the guy that seconds the motion, is
The "Remarkable Dr. Eells."

So this place should stand forever,
Never leaning on its heels
For that's the way he's lived his life
The "remarkable Dr. Eells."

5. Editorial in *Walton Reporter*, in mid-1970s

For Man of the Year

It is hoped the result of last week's school election will not deter other well-qualified young fathers and mothers from seeking a position on the school board.

The vote last Tuesday was simply a recognition that Dr. Walter E. Eells, who was a candidate for a fifth term on the board, is a man who has deservedly won a high place in the esteem of the community. There is probably no one else in the area who commands the respect and admiration of so many people.

Dr. Eells is a busy man who has always had a large medical practice and there are few of his patients who do not have an intense loyalty but this alone is not the reason for his popularity. He has also taken a prominent part in community life. In addition to his long term on the board of education, he has served for a long period as one of the trustees of Ogden Free Library. He is a firm supporter of his church. He gives liberally to any project for the improvement of this community.

The Carrie Eells Smith Nursing home, which he conducts, furnishes a needed home for the aged and infirm. In a quiet manner he has probably done more for the area than any other man still alive.

Each year Walton Chamber of Commerce has named a man of the year but the committee in charge of that function has not gone outside the mercantile and business area to select a qualified nominee. Our nominee for the next man of the year is Dr. Eells.

We also trust that Duane Merrill, the young farmer who sought a seat on the board this year, will not be disheartened by his defeat. He ran against a candidate who is unbeatable.

6. **Card from Margaret A. Tweedie, who retired, then worked another quarter of a century for her neighbor on Townsend Street.**

Dear Dr. Eells—

A terrific boss—working for you was one of the best things that ever happened to me... I thought I was going to be with you until you retired, but that did not happen. You have always had time for me since I left there. In no way can I tell you what the calls and cards have meant to me over the years when you were out of town. I am truly grateful—it makes such a difference. I am looking forward to your continued thoughtfulness. I love you. (M.A.T.)

Tributes on the anniversary of Dad's 60 years in medicine and his 90th birthday

1. **Betty and Maynard Elderkin**

Dear Dr. Eells,

We congratulate you on all these many years of being the best Dr. in Walton. You have to read all this because it tells you how I (Betty) really feel about you. You were the one who delivered our children with such care—and when they were sick always made them well for us. I do remember when I was "delivering" Jack and that was March 21st, 1948, and also at our anniversary you said, "you have 20 minutes left to have this baby on your anniversary." I groaned and said there are things I'd rather be doing about now, how you laughed and guess what—3 minutes before 12 he was born.

There were bad times when I needed surgery and wasn't scared if you were there. I always trusted you to care for me and you did.

There were times when money was very scarce and you always waited—there aren't enough words to ever tell you how we both feel about you!

May God grant you more years here with us and when He takes you, we know heavens gates will open wide to welcome a wonderful doctor and friend into His heavenly home—and everyone here will always remember all the good years with you!

We appreciate you and love you so very much.

2. Nancy Michel

25 August 1996

Dear Dr. Eells,

When I think about the person who has had the greatest impact on my life (other than my parents), your name comes immediately to mind. On April 14, 1949, you delivered me in Smith Hospital. I don't remember much about that—so I'll have to take my Mom's word for it.

I do remember, though, the day you took out my tonsils. I was five then and I was scared, but you assured me there was nothing to worry about. Just a sore throat that would soon heal and I could eat all the ice cream I wanted in the meantime. The ether made me sick and I saw a scary 'spring man' in my dreams, but soon it was all over. And you were right! I was soon as good as new, minus my tonsils and a few pounds heavier thanks to the ice cream.

I also remember the many shots I had in your back office when it was time to go to school. I dreaded those, but seldom cried because I liked to hear you say what a 'big girl' I was. So I just gritted my teeth and cried afterwards.

There was another time I was glad you were there. I was allergic to hay and in the summer when they mowed it in back of our house my throat would close up so I could hardly breathe. I would panic. And Mom would take me to see you and you always knew how to make it better. (Oxygen, I think, through a funny mask.) I finally outgrew that, just like you said I would.

Then there was the night I was twelve, and had such bad stomach pains I couldn't sleep and I kept throwing up. Next morning in your office, there was no doubt. "We've got to take it out now," you said. And we barely had time. I was really glad to see you that day. When it was over, you put me in a room with a lady who was a comedienne, and I thought I'd burst my stitches. Since then, I've avoided wearing bikinis because of my big scar, but I don't care; I see it as a symbol of someone who loved me and took care of me.

Finally, I was 'grown' and graduated from high school, on my way to becoming a teacher. It was you who offered me my first job that summer. I didn't mind I had to empty bedpans and mop the floors, I loved taking care of the old people in Smith Nursing Home. I was introduced to death there, but also learned a lot about life. I want to thank you on your birthday for all the times you played a major role in my life. I will never forget you. Happy Birthday.

3. Betsy (Web) Munn

7-18-90

Dear Dr. Eells,

I'm late but I just want to say congratulations on being a wonderful Dr. for 60 years.

I know you delivered me and my first child. I remember calling you when I was in labor and Mrs. Eells said you were at the basketball game, so I waited at home for you to return. Not wanting to go without you.

Then there was the time when Dad got hit by a car while crossing Delaware Street. He went first to you and you told him he had a fracture, but you sent him over for X-rays. Of course the X-rays showed just what you said. Then when he was recovering at home you made house calls on him just to see how he was doing. I don't know of another Dr. that would have done that.

There also have been the times when I've interrupted a few meals and held you up when you were leaving to go somewhere. You never refused to see us.

I can go on and on with memories of things that you have done for us—but to sum it all up I'm so proud and grateful to have you for our Dr.

Thank you for being there.

4. Betsy and Rick Weidenback

Dr. Eells -

You're one doctor we enjoy coming to see cause you care for our ailments but also provide some interesting or amusing conversation about past, present or future!

As a little girl I remember running laps around your office when you were checking my heart murmur & you and my dad got talking—I think I did 100 laps!! And in present days it's me forgetting the time as we discuss the history of East Brook's famous or when Rick comes in with an earache: we interrupt your Sunday evenin' scrabble game or finish a Hogan's Heroes show & discuss those while you ably remedy the ills!

You're great—Congratulations—we're blessed to have such an old-time doctor to see!

Actually you are <u>incredible</u>, but I don't want you getting a big head or anything!

60 Years of PRACTICE! <u>BRAVO</u>!

5. Letter from Geoffrey and Lisa Gray (and Christy)

Dear Grandpap:

Congratulations! Sixty years is certainly commendable. I'm quite sure the people whose lives you touched feel that they are better because of having had contact with you. It would be enjoyable sitting down with you for a few hours to hear you describe how the medical profession has changed over the last sixty years; let's do that some time.

Well, grandpap, may the next sixty be as enjoyable as the last sixty.

Good luck and have a wonderful day.

Two different samples of Dad's writing

1. **A short story written for the Walton Central High School publication, Our Tattler, in 1921. I'm not sure if it's fact or fiction or a little of both. I'll let the reader decide.**

A RABBIT HUNT

One day last winter my grandfather asked me to go hunting with him on the following day, which was Friday. I was very glad to go and told him so. It was agreed upon that we were to start early in the morning and go on the hills around Deposit. We were to take two guns and my dog with us.

We started very early and walked for miles. I soon tired out but said nothing to my grandfather. Gip went ahead of us and looked at everything, smelled of everything and barked at everything. My grandfather soon noticed that Gip stopped near a large pile of brush. He called my attention to him and said, "A rabbit is in there." Suddenly Gip gave a loud bark and jumped on the pile. Instantly a large rabbit jumped from under the pile and ran like lightning toward the woods, which were a few rods away.

"Run after it!" yelled grandfather. I ran through berry bushes and over dead branches of trees till my breath gave out and then I stopped. I must have run a long way from grandfather for when I stopped I didn't know where I was. I wandered around for a while and then I sat down under a large pine tree. Suddenly a few drops of rain, which fell on my outstretched hand, startled me. It rained and rained and I began to think it never would stop. The rain froze about as soon as it fell. When I began to think that the rain on me would freeze, I got up from under the tree and started north. Suddenly from under my feet there came a loud "caw" and I jumped back. Right in front of me was a large crow. I stood, for a moment frightened, but I soon was all right. I slowly started for the crow but it hopped away. Every time I got anywhere near he would hop away. At last I was out of patience with him and jumped. When I landed his right wing was under my feet.

I picked him up and found that his wing was broken and that was the reason that he couldn't fly away. I held his bill together with my fingers and started to go north again. I didn't remember ever being here before and I soon realized that I was lost. I wandered around for a long time and at last gave up and sat down on a rotten log to think.

Suddenly at my right I heard the sound of a gun. "Bang, Bang!" it went. I jumped from the log and ran toward the place where the sound came. As I ran through some bushes in front of me, I saw my grandfather holding two rabbits in his hand. He didn't know where I had been when the storm came up. He had hidden in a cave when the storm came and when it stopped he had continued hunting. That night when we arrived home, we had a live crow and two dead rabbits to show the people.

2. **Dad kept in close touch for several years in the 1960s, with some of the medical students who worked with him during the summers. They were usually written to (Dr.) Bill Willard who was asked to share them with others. They are a remarkable combination of medical details and family/local history. Here's proof.**

2 Oct. 1960

Dear Bill:

Thought you would like to know about some of the cases you saw with me last weekend.

We were glad you had a pleasant visit to Walton. We were pleased with the reunion, at any rate, and hope you fellows can come back another weekend. X-mas would be a good time, if you have some time off and it isn't all spoken for. We will be looking for you the last week in August. Be sure to let us know when to meet you in Deposit, Sidney, or whatnot.

Mr. Bristol in Room 5, on the right, the 80-year-old, was something of a surprise when his tissue report came back. It read: infiltrating adenocarcinoma of cecum, as well as lymphosarcoma of the cecum with involvement of regional lymph glands. I have talked things over with the surgeon (Dr. Polley) and the X-ray man at Del. Valley Hosp. and I think I'll try some Nitrogen mustard on him.

You remember the Luehmann boy who came back from N.J. because of the stomach ache? We did him the day after you left Walton. I was surprised that he had a fairly acute appendix. His report was a surprise, too: acute appendicitis and carcinoid of appendix. My <u>first</u> carcinoid. I had read of carcinoids but never ran across one before.

We did the 20-year-old gal Monday after you left: had one mulberry stone & 20-30 tiny irregular stones; as well as many adhesions around the gallbladder. We did the old gal across the hall, "Aunt Rachel" on Friday. Had a big gallbladder, full of thick black bile; she had a definitely stenosed cystic duct. She is doing well.

The subtotal gastrectomy we did last Tuesday is good. He was out in the hall today, receiving visitors.

Had an active duodenal ulcer come in 2 days ago. X-rays scheduled for next Tuesday. Have a hernia scheduled for next Friday. Old fellow coming in tomorrow for biopsy of ear—definite cancer.

The little girl with the pelvic mass went home last night. The I.V.P. showed the lower third of the left ureter was displaced toward the midline. The B.E. showed compression of the rectosigmoid & distal loop of the sigmoid by some circular mass, size of golfball—X-ray dept. won't commit itself: could be something retroperitoneal, or in broad ligament, or possibly left ovary. Dr. Polley thinks it came from abscessed appendix. I think it more likely came from Meckel's diverticulum. Her temp came down, she has no soreness, the mass is definitely on the left (on rectal examination), firm, nontender. I thought I could find a little soft spot in it, when I checked her yesterday before she went home. She is to come back for weekly checkup, etc.

The boy with the metastatic osteogenic sarcoma on the left arm, left chest, etc., is slipping fast. Calls for hypo about every 2 hours. Getting rather pale and weak.

On the 12th a 29-year-old came in with black stools. He had a splenectomy in 1948. Shunt in 1950. Dr. Blakemore did both. I presume you have heard of him. In 1958 he fell from a silo & got a nasty fracture of the ankle and a compression fracture of L 2 (or maybe L 1). He did a lot of bleeding following that fall. On July 15th he fell backwards and landed on his back on the edge of a concrete platform. Jarred his old spinal fracture a little. On Aug. 11th he started to have tarry stools again. <u>He</u> blames the bleeding on his fall some 3 weeks previously. I can't see the connection, can you? He had 2 units of blood. Normal stool today. He is determined to go home tomorrow—has to go to the Del. Co. Fair, at Walton! Big time, with harness racing, tractor pulling, etc., etc.

I didn't intend to make this so long when I started it. But I got rambling on, and here I am near the middle of the second page.

It didn't quiet down much after you left. Monday some friends from Grand Rapids arrived, 2 adults & 3 children. Former pastor who left Walton 4 years ago. Quite young couple. We prefer younger people, apparently, because we are getting older and want young folk around to make us feel young again, or something. They were here 4 days. Next day (Friday) another former pastor & wife, now in Beaver Falls, Pa., arrived, after a trip to Maine. We are fortunate to have a cabin in the country. We park our company there when we got an overflow. Some prefer to stay there. 5 miles from town. Can hear the brook babble under the bedroom window, that is, if there is a brook. The other day we had a picnic at the cabin and there was no water in the brook. Seems odd, for we have had a very wet summer.

It is after one a.m. Time to get the mail off. Then a few hours sleep.

I doubt if I'll get around to writing Bill Anderson this time. You can pass the letter along for him to read, if you like. Maybe I should have made a carbon copy for him! I have been known to do that. Mrs. Eells doesn't think much of it.

Again, we would be happy to have you come up for a visit before you go back to school. Just let us know when & where to meet you.

ABOUT THE AUTHOR

Robert J Eells, is Professor of History and Political Science at Spring Arbor College in Michigan. He has taught for twenty-six years—previously at Geneva College in Pennsylvania, Rockmont College in Colorado, and at Trinity Christian College in Illinois. Professor Eells has his B.S. from Geneva College, an M.A. from Union College in New York State, and a Ph.D. from the University of New Mexico in American Studies. Dr. Eells is the author of two previous biographies—*Lonely Walk: the Life of Senator Mark O. Hatfield* (1979) and *Forgotten Saint: the Life of Theodore Frelinghuysen* (1987). He is also the author of about twenty articles—mostly about religion and politics—and a dozen book reviews.

Because his father—Walter E. Eells—had his medical office right in his home and his own hospital across the street, many of the stories in Country Doctor were witnessed by his son, Robert, or were related directly to him by other family members, friends, or long-time patients. And because the author for a time considered medicine as a vocation, he "experienced" some of these stories existentially by assuming the role of a young "Dr. Kildare" during the 1960s—as a high school and college student. As a result, he was privileged to witness and experience a type of medicine which—sadly but understandably—no longer exists.

Dr. Eells is married to Janice (Johnson) formerly of Albuquerque, New Mexico and they have two children—Richard (14) and Anne (11).

Printed in the United States
5580